The Poetry of Edmund Waller

Volume I

Edmund Waller, FRS was born on March 3rd, 1606 in Coleshill, Buckinghamshire.

Waller was educated at the Royal Grammar School, High Wycombe and thence on to Eton and King's College, Cambridge. His adult life is very colourful and displays a man whose adventures and experiences made poetry an obvious vessel to express the journey.

He entered Parliament early, at age 18, and was, at first, an active member of the opposition. (Waller was to sit in Parliament at various times from 1624-1679) In 1631 he married a London heiress, a surreptitious marriage to a wealthy ward of the Court of Aldermen. Waller was brought before the Star Chamber for this offence, and heavily fined. Waller was however, a wealthy man and stayed so throughout his life despite the many fines he became liable for.

His wife bore him a son and a daughter at Beaconsfield but died in 1634.

After her death he unsuccessfully courted Lady Dorothy Sidney, the 'Sacharissa' of his poems.

By 1643 he had now switched sides to the Royalists and was the leader in the plot to seize London for Charles I, which is known as "Waller's Plot". On 30 May he and his friends were arrested. In the terror of discovery, Waller confessed "whatever he had said heard, thought or seen, and all that he knew... or suspected of others". His fellow conspirators were far braver and were unwilling to betray their principles or each other.

Waller was called before the bar of the House in July, and made an abject and complete speech of recantation. His life was spared and he was committed to the Tower of London, but, on paying a fine of £10,000, he was released and banished from the realm in November 1643.

It was now, in 1644 that he married Mary Bracey and together they took up residence at Rouen. She went on to bear him several children.

In 1646 Waller travelled with John Evelyn to Switzerland and Italy.

He made his peace with Cromwell in 1651 and returned to England but was only restored to favour with Cromwell's death and the Restoration of Charles II.

By now experience had taught him to keep all sides happy. Accordingly as he wrote poetic tributes to both Oliver Cromwell (1655) and Charles II (1660).

A precocious poet; he began to write, it is thought, in his late teens with a complimentary piece on His Majesty's Escape at St Andere written using the heroic couplet. Interestingly throughout his writing career he rejected the dense and intellectual verse of Metaphysical poetry. His more relaxed style helped prepare the way for the emergence of the heroic couplet. By the end of the 17th century it had become the dominant form of English poetry. His style is beguiling and of a polished simplicity. The great John Dryden thought him, along with Sir John Denham, as poets who brought about the Augustan age.

Edmund Waller died on October 21st, 1687 at the age of 81. He is buried at St Mary and All Saints Church, Beaconsfield

Index of Contents

MISCELLANEOUS POEMS

OF THE DANGER HIS MAJESTY [BEING PRINCE] ESCAPED IN THE ROAD AT ST ANDERO [1]

Now bad his Highness bid farewell to Spain,
And reach'd the sphere of his own power—the main;
With British bounty in his ship he feasts
Th' Hesperian princes, his amazed guests,
To find that watery wilderness exceed
The entertainment of their great Madrid.
Healths to both kings, attended with the roar
Of cannons, echo'd from th'affrighted shore,
With loud resemblance of his thunder, prove
Bacchus the seed of cloud-compelling Jove;
While to his harp divine Arion sings[2]

The loves and conquests of our Albion kings.

Of the Fourth Edward was his noble song,
Fierce, goodly, valiant, beautiful, and young;
He rent the crown from vanquish'd Henry's head,
Raised the White Rose, and trampled on the Red;
Till love, triumphing o'er the victor's pride,
Brought Mars and Warwick to the conquer'd side:
Neglected Warwick (whose bold hand, like Fate,
Gives and resumes the sceptre of our state)
Woos for his master; and with double shame,
Himself deluded, mocks the princely dame,
The Lady Bona, whom just anger burns,
And foreign war with civil rage returns.
Ah! spare your swords, where beauty is to blame;
Love gave th'affront, and must repair the same;
When France shall boast of her, whose conqu'ring eyes
Have made the best of English hearts their prize;
Have power to alter the decrees of Fate,
And change again the counsels of our state.
What the prophetic Muse intends, alone
To him that feels the secret wound is known.
With the sweet sound of this harmonious lay,
About the keel delighted dolphins play,
Too sure a sign of sea's ensuing rage,
Which must anon this royal troop engage;
To whom soft sleep seems more secure and sweet,
Within the town commanded by our fleet.
These mighty peers placed in the gilded barge,
Proud with the burden of so brave a charge,
With painted oars the youths begin to sweep
Neptune's smooth face, and cleave the yielding deep;
Which soon becomes the seat of sudden war
Between the wind and tide that fiercely jar.
As when a sort[3] of lusty shepherds try
Their force at football, care of victory
Makes them salute so rudely breast to breast,
That their encounter seems too rough for jest;
They ply their feet, and still the restless ball,
Toss'd to and fro, is urged by them all:
So fares the doubtful barge 'twixt tide and winds,
And like effect of their contention finds.
Yet the bold Britons still securely row'd;
Charles and his virtue was their sacred load;
Than which a greater pledge Heaven could not give,
That the good boat this tempest should outlive.
But storms increase, and now no hope of grace
Among them shines, save in the Prince's face;

The rest resign their courage, skill, and sight,
To danger, horror, and unwelcome night.
The gentle vessel (wont with state and pride
On the smooth back of silver Thames to ride)
Wanders astonish'd in the angry main,
As Titan's car did, while the golden rein
Fill'd the young hand of his adventurous son,[4]
When the whole world an equal hazard run
To this of ours, the light of whose desire
Waves threaten now, as that was scared by fire.
Th' impatient sea grows impotent, and raves,
That, night assisting, his impetuous waves
Should find resistance from so light a thing;
These surges ruin, those our safety bring.
Th' oppress'd vessel doth the charge abide,
Only because assail'd on every side;
So men with rage and passion set on fire,
Trembling for haste, impeach their mad desire.

The pale Iberians had expired with fear,
But that their wonder did divert their care,
To see the Prince with danger moved no more
Than with the pleasures of their court before;
Godlike his courage seem'd, whom nor delight
Could soften, nor the face of death affright.
Next to the power of making tempests cease,
Was in that storm to have so calm a peace.
Great Maro could no greater tempest feign,
When the loud winds usurping on the main,
For angry Juno labour'd to destroy
The hated relics of confounded Troy;
His bold Aeneas, on like billows toss'd
In a tall ship, and all his country lost,
Dissolves with fear; and both his hands upheld,
Proclaims them happy whom the Greeks had quell'd
In honourable fight; our hero, set
In a small shallop, Fortune in his debt,
So near a hope of crowns and sceptres, more
Than ever Priam, when he flourish'd, wore;
His loins yet full of ungot princes, all
His glory in the bud, lets nothing fall
That argues fear; if any thought annoys
The gallant youth, 'tis love's untasted joys,
And dear remembrance of that fatal glance,
For which he lately pawn'd his heart[5] in France;
Where he had seen a brighter nymph than she[6]
That sprung out of his present foe, the sea.
That noble ardour, more than mortal fire,

The conquer'd ocean could not make expire;
Nor angry Thetis raise her waves above
Th' heroic Prince's courage or his love;
'Twas indignation, and not fear he felt,
The shrine should perish where that image dwelt.
Ah, Love forbid! the noblest of thy train
Should not survive to let her know his pain;
Who nor his peril minding, nor his flame,
Is entertain'd with some less serious game,
Among the bright nymphs of the Gallic court,
All highly born, obsequious to her sport;
They roses seem, which in their early pride
But half reveal, and half their beauties hide;
She the glad morning, which her beams does throw
Upon their smiling leaves, and gilds them so;
Like bright Aurora, whose refulgent ray
Foretells the fervour of ensuing day,
And warns the shepherd with his flocks retreat
To leafy shadows from the threaten'd heat.

From Cupid's string, of many shafts that fled
Wing'd with those plumes which noble Fame had shed,
As through the wond'ring world she flew, and told
Of his adventures, haughty, brave, and bold,
Some had already touch'd the royal maid,
But Love's first summons seldom are obey'd;
Light was the wound, the Prince's care unknown,
She might not, would not, yet reveal her own.
His glorious name had so possess'd her ears,
That with delight those antique tales she hears
Of Jason, Theseus, and such worthies old,
As with his story best resemblance hold.
And now she views, as on the wall it hung,
What old Musæus so divinely sung;
Which art with life and love did so inspire,
That she discerns and favours that desire,
Which there provokes th'advent'rous youth to swim,
And in Leander's danger pities him;
Whose not new love alone, but fortune, seeks
To frame his story like that amorous Greek's.

For from the stern of some good ship appears
A friendly light, which moderates their fears;
New courage from reviving hope they take,
And climbing o'er the waves that taper make,
On which the hope of all their lives depends,
As his on that fair Hero's hand extends.
The ship at anchor, like a fixed rock,

Breaks the proud billows which her large sides knock;
Whose rage restrainèd, foaming higher swells,
And from her port the weary barge repels,
Threat'ning to make her, forcèd out again,
Repeat the dangers of the troubled main.
Twice was the cable hurl'd in vain; the Fates
Would not be movèd for our sister states;
For England is the third successful throw,
And then the genius of that land they know,
Whose prince must be (as their own books devise)
Lord of the scene where now his danger lies.

Well sung the Roman bard, 'All human things
Of dearest value hang on slender strings.'
Oh, see the then sole hope, and, in design
Of Heaven, our joy, supported by a line!
Which for that instant was Heaven's care above
The chain that's fixèd to the throne of Jove,
On which the fabric of our world depends;
One link dissolved, the whole creation ends.

FOOTNOTES

[1] 'St. Andero': St. Andrews. He had newly abandoned his suit for the Infanta.—
[2] 'Arion sings': Alluding to the deliverance of Charles I., on his return from Spain, from a violent storm in the Bay of Biscay, October 1623.
[3] 'Sort': a company.
[4] 'Adventurous son': Phaeton.
[5] Henrietta, afterwards Queen.
[6] Venus.

OF HIS MAJESTY'S RECEIVING THE NEWS OF THE DUKE OF BUCKINGHAM'S DEATH

So earnest with thy God! can no new care,
No sense of danger, interrupt thy prayer?
The sacred wrestler, till a blessing given,
Quits not his hold, but halting conquers Heaven;
Nor was the stream of thy devotion stopp'd,
When from the body such a limb was lopp'd,
As to thy present state was no less maim,
Though thy wise choice has since repair'd the same.
Bold Homer durst not so great virtue feign
In his best pattern:[2] of Patroclus slain,
With such amazement as weak mothers use,
And frantic gesture, he receives the news.
Yet fell his darling by th'impartial chance
Of war, imposed by royal Hector's lance;

Thine, in full peace, and by a vulgar hand
Torn from thy bosom, left his high command.

The famous painter[3] could allow no place
For private sorrow in a prince's face:
Yet, that his piece might not exceed belief,
He cast a veil upon supposed grief.
'Twas want of such a precedent as this
Made the old heathen frame their gods amiss.
Their Phoebus should not act a fonder part
For the fair boy,[4] than he did for his heart;
Nor blame for Hyacinthus' fate his own,
That kept from him wish'd death, hadst thou been known.

He that with thine shall weigh good David's deeds,
Shall find his passion, nor his love, exceeds:
He cursed the mountains where his brave friend died,
But let false Ziba with his heir divide;
Where thy immortal love to thy bless'd friends,
Like that of Heaven, upon their seed descends.
Such huge extremes inhabit thy great mind,
Godlike, unmoved, and yet, like woman, kind!
Which of the ancient poets had not brought
Our Charles's pedigree from Heaven, and taught
How some bright dame, compress'd by mighty Jove,
Produced this mix'd Divinity and Love?

FOOTNOTES

[1] 'Buckingham's death': Buckingham was murdered by Felton at Portsmouth, on the 23d of August 1628, while equipping a fleet for the relief of Rochelle. Lord Lindsey succeeded him. The king was at prayers when the news arrived, and had the resolution to disguise his emotion till they were over.
[2] 'Pattern': Achilles.
[3] 'Painter': Timanthes in his picture of Iphigenia.
[4] 'Fair boy': Cyparissus.

ON THE TAKING OF SALLÈ [1]

Of Jason, Theseus, and such worthies old,
Light seem the tales antiquity has told;
Such beasts and monsters as their force oppress'd,
Some places only, and some times, infest.
Sallè, that scorn'd all power and laws of men,
Goods with their owners hurrying to their den,
And future ages threat'ning with a rude
And savage race, successively renew'd;
Their king despising with rebellious pride,

And foes profess'd to all the world beside;
This pest of mankind gives our hero fame,
And through the obliged world dilates his name.
The prophet once to cruel Agag said,
'As thy fierce sword has mothers childless made,
So shall the sword make thine;' and with that word
He hew'd the man in pieces with his sword.

Just Charles like measure has return'd to these
Whose Pagan hands had stain'd the troubled seas;
With ships they made the spoiled merchant mourn;
With ships their city and themselves are torn.
One squadron of our winged castles sent,
O'erthrew their fort, and all their navy rent;
For, not content the dangers to increase,
And act the part of tempests in the seas,
Like hungry wolves, those pirates from our shore
Whole flocks of sheep, and ravish'd cattle bore.
Safely they might on other nations prey—
Fools to provoke the sovereign of the sea!
Mad Cacus so, whom like ill fate persuades,
The herd of fair Alcmena's seed invades,
Who for revenge, and mortals' glad relief,
Sack'd the dark cave and crush'd that horrid thief.

Morocco's monarch, wond'ring at this fact,
Save that his presence his affairs exact,
Had come in person to have seen and known
The injured world's revenger and his own.
Hither he sends the chief among his peers,
Who in his bark proportion'd presents bears,
To the renown'd for piety and force,
Poor captives manumised, and matchless horse.[2]

FOOTNOTES
[1] 'Sallè': Sallè, a town of Fez, given to piracy, was taken and destroyed in 1632 by the army of the Emperor of Morocco, assisted by some English vessels.
[2] 'Horse': the Emperor of Morocco, in gratitude to Charles, sent him a present of Barbary horses, and three hundred manumitted Christian slaves.—

That shipwreck'd vessel which th'Apostle bore,
Scarce suffer'd more upon Melita's shore,
Than did his temple in the sea of time,
Our nation's glory, and our nation's crime.

When the first monarch[2] of this happy isle,
Moved with the ruin of so brave a pile,
This work of cost and piety begun,
To be accomplish'd by his glorious son,
Who all that came within the ample thought
Of his wise sire has to perfection brought;
He, like Amphion, makes those quarries leap
Into fair figures from a confused heap;
For in his art of regiment is found
A power like that of harmony in sound.

Those antique minstrels, sure, were Charles-like kings,
Cities their lutes, and subjects' hearts their strings,
On which with so divine a hand they strook,
Consent of motion from their breath they took:
So all our minds with his conspire to grace
The Gentiles' great Apostle, and deface
Those state-obscuring sheds, that like a chain
Seem'd to confine and fetter him again;
Which the glad saint shakes off at his command,
As once the viper from his sacred hand:
So joys the aged oak, when we divide
The creeping ivy from his injured side.

Ambition rather would affect the fame
Of some new structure, to have borne her name.
Two distant virtues in one act we find,
The modesty and greatness of his mind;
Which, not content to be above the rage,
And injury of all-impairing age,
In its own worth secure, doth higher climb,
And things half swallow'd from the jaws of Time

Reduce; an earnest of his grand design,
To frame no new church, but the old refine;
Which, spouse-like, may with comely grace command,
More than by force of argument or hand.
For doubtful reason few can apprehend,
And war brings ruin where it should amend;
But beauty, with a bloodless conquest finds
A welcome sovereignty in rudest minds.

Not aught which Sheba's wond'ring queen beheld
Amongst the works of Solomon, excell'd
His ships and building; emblems of a heart
Large both in magnanimity and art.

While the propitious heavens this work attend,

Long-wanted showers they forget to send;
As if they meant to make it understood
Of more importance than our vital food.

The sun, which riseth to salute the quire
Already finished, setting shall admire
How private bounty could so far extend:
The King built all, but Charles the western end.[3]
So proud a fabric to devotion given,
At once it threatens and obliges Heaven!

Laomedon, that had the gods in pay,
Neptune, with him that rules the sacred day,[4]
Could no such structure raise: Troy wall'd so high,
Th' Atrides might as well have forced the sky.

Glad, though amazed, are our neighbour kings,
To see such power employ'd in peaceful things;
They list not urge it to the dreadful field;
The task is easier to destroy than build.

... Sic gratia regum
Pieriis tentam modis...—HORACE.

FOOTNOTES

[1] 'St. Paul's': these repairs commenced in the spring of 1633.
[2] 'Monarch': King James I.
[3] 'Western end': the western end, built at Charles' own expense, consisted of a splendid portico, built by Inigo Jones.
[4] 'Sacred day': Apollo.

THE COUNTESS OF CARLISLE IN MOURNING [1]

When from black clouds no part of sky is clear,
But just so much as lets the sun appear,
Heaven then would seem thy image, and reflect
Those sable vestments, and that bright aspect.
A spark of virtue by the deepest shade
Of sad adversity is fairer made;
Nor less advantage doth thy beauty get,
A Venus rising from a sea of jet!
Such was th'appearance of new-formed light,
While yet it struggled with eternal night.
Then mourn no more, lest thou admit increase
Of glory by thy noble lord's decease.
We find not that the laughter-loving dame[2]

Mourn'd for Anchises; 'twas enough she came
To grace the mortal with her deathless bed,
And that his living eyes such beauty fed;
Had she been there, untimely joy, through all
Men's hearts diffused, had marr'd the funeral.
Those eyes were made to banish grief: as well
Bright Phoebus might affect in shades to dwell,
As they to put on sorrow: nothing stands,
But power to grieve, exempt from thy commands.
If thou lament, thou must do so alone;
Grief in thy presence can lay hold on none.
Yet still persist the memory to love
Of that great Mercury of our mighty Jove,
Who, by the power of his enchanting tongue,
Swords from the hands of threat'ning monarchs wrung.
War he prevented, or soon made it cease,
Instructing princes in the arts of peace;
Such as made Sheba's curious queen resort
To the large-hearted Hebrew's famous court.
Had Homer sat amongst his wond'ring guests,
He might have learn'd at those stupendous feasts,
With greater bounty, and more sacred state,
The banquets of the gods to celebrate.
But oh! what elocution might he use,
What potent charms, that could so soon infuse
His absent master's love into the heart
Of Henrietta! forcing her to part
From her loved brother, country, and the sun,
And, like Camilla, o'er the waves to run
Into his arms! while the Parisian dames
Mourn for the ravish'd glory; at her flames
No less amazed than the amazèd stars,
When the bold charmer of Thessalia wars
With Heaven itself, and numbers does repeat,
Which call descending Cynthia from her seat.

FOOTNOTES

[1] 'Mourning': Carlisle was a luxurious liver, and died in 1636, poor, but, like many spendthrifts, popular.
He had represented Prince Charles at his marriage with Princess Henrietta at Paris.
[2] 'Dame': Venus.

I

What fury has provoked thy wit to dare,
With Diomede, to wound the Queen of Love?

Thy mistress' envy, or thine own despair?
Not the just Pallas in thy breast did move
So blind a rage, with such a diff'rent fate;
He honour won, where thou hast purchased hate.

II
She gave assistance to his Trojan foe;
Thou, that without a rival thou may'st love,
Dost to the beauty of this lady owe,
While after her the gazing world does move.
Canst thou not be content to love alone?
Or is thy mistress not content with one?

III
Hast thou not read of Fairy Arthur's shield,
Which, but disclosed, amazed the weaker eyes
Of proudest foes, and won the doubtful field?
So shall thy rebel wit become her prize.
Should thy iambics swell into a book,
All were confuted with one radiant look.

IV
Heaven he obliged that placed her in the skies;
Rewarding Phoebus, for inspiring so
His noble brain, by likening to those eyes
His joyful beams; but Phoebus is thy foe,
And neither aids thy fancy nor thy sight,
So ill thou rhym'st against so fair a light.

OF HER CHAMBER

They taste of death that do at heaven arrive;
But we this paradise approach alive.
Instead of death, the dart of love does strike,
And renders all within these walls alike.
The high in titles, and the shepherd, here
Forgets his greatness, and forgets his fear.
All stand amazed, and gazing on the fair,
Lose thought of what themselves or others are;
Ambition lose, and have no other scope,
Save Carlisle's favour, to employ their hope.
The Thracian[1] could (though all those tales were true
The bold Greeks tell) no greater wonders do;
Before his feet so sheep and lions lay,
Fearless and wrathless while they heard him play.
The gay, the wise, the gallant, and the grave,

Subdued alike, all but one passion have;
No worthy mind but finds in hers there is
Something proportion'd to the rule of his;
While she with cheerful, but impartial grace,
(Born for no one, but to delight the race
Of men) like Phoebus so divides her light,
And warms us, that she stoops not from her height.

FOOTNOTE
[1] 'Thracian': Orpheus.—

THYRSIS, GALATEA [1]

THYRSIS.
As lately I on silver Thames did ride,
Sad Galatea on the bank I spied;
Such was her look as sorrow taught to shine,
And thus she graced me with a voice divine.

GALATEA.
You that can tune your sounding strings so well,
Of ladies' beauties, and of love to tell,
Once change your note, and let your lute report
The justest grief that ever touch'd the Court.

THYRSIS.
Fair nymph! I have in your delights no share,
Nor ought to be concerned in your care;
Yet would I sing if I your sorrows knew,
And to my aid invoke no Muse but you.

GALATEA.
Hear then, and let your song augment our grief,
Which is so great as not to wish relief.
She that had all which Nature gives, or Chance,
Whom Fortune join'd with Virtue to advance
To all the joys this island could afford,
The greatest mistress, and the kindest lord;
Who with the royal mix'd her noble blood,
And in high grace with Gloriana[2] stood;
Her bounty, sweetness, beauty, goodness, such,
That none e'er thought her happiness too much;
So well-inclined her favours to confer,
And kind to all, as Heaven had been to her!
The virgin's part, the mother, and the wife,
So well she acted in this span of life,

That though few years (too flew, alas!) she told,
She seem'd in all things, but in beauty, old.
As unripe fruit, whose verdant stalks do cleave
Close to the tree, which grieves no less to leave
The smiling pendant which adorns her so,
And until autumn on the bough should grow;
So seem'd her youthful soul not eas'ly forced,
Or from so fair, so sweet a seat divorced.
Her fate at once did hasty seem and slow;
At once too cruel, and unwilling too.

THYRSIS.
Under how hard a law are mortals born!
Whom now we envy, we anon must mourn;
What Heaven sets highest, and seems most to prize,
Is soon removed from our wond'ring eyes!
But since the Sisters[3] did so soon untwine
So fair a thread, I'll strive to piece the line.
Vouchsafe, sad nymph! to let me know the dame,
And to the Muses I'll commend her name;
Make the wide country echo to your moan,
The list'ning trees and savage mountains groan.
What rock's not movèd when the death is sung
Of one so good, so lovely, and so young?

GALATEA.
'Twas Hamilton!—whom I had named before,
But naming her, grief lets me say no more.

FOOTNOTES
[1] 'Galatea': the lady here mourned was the Duchess of Hamilton, a niece of Buckingham; she died in
1638.
[2] 'Gloriana': Queen Henrietta.
[3] 'Sisters': Parcæ—

ON MY LADY DOROTHY SIDNEY'S PICTURE [1]

Such was Philoclea, and such Dorus' flame!
The matchless Sidney, that immortal frame
Of perfect beauty on two pillars placed,
Not his high fancy could one pattern, graced
With such extremes of excellence, compose;
Wonders so distant in one face disclose!
Such cheerful modesty, such humble state,
Moves certain love, but with as doubtful fate
As when, beyond our greedy reach, we see

Inviting fruit on too sublime a tree.
All the rich flowers through his Arcadia found,
Amazed we see in this one garland bound.
Had but this copy (which the artist took
From the fair picture of that noble book)
Stood at Kalander's, the brave friends had jarr'd,
And, rivals made, th'ensuing story marr'd.
Just nature, first instructed by his thought,
In his own house thus practised what he taught;
This glorious piece transcends what he could think,
So much his blood is nobler than his ink![2]

FOOTNOTES

[1] 'Dorothy Sidney': see Life for an account of 'Saccharissa.'
[2] 'Philoclea and Dorus': the reader may turn for these names and their histories, to the glorious, flowery wilderness of the 'Arcadia.' Sidney was granduncle to Dorothy.

AT PENSHURST

Had Dorothea lived when mortals made
Choice of their deities, this sacred shade
Had held an altar to her power, that gave
The peace and glory which these alleys have;
Embroider'd so with flowers where she stood,
That it became a garden of a wood.
Her presence has such more than human grace,
That it can civilise the rudest place;
And beauty too, and order, can impart,
Where nature ne'er intended it, nor art.
The plants acknowledge this, and her admire,
No less than those of old did Orpheus' lyre;
If she sit down, with tops all tow'rds her bow'd,
They round about her into arbours crowd;
Or if she walk, in even ranks they stand,
Like some well-marshall'd and obsequious band.
Amphion so made stones and timber leap
Into fair figures from a confused heap;
And in the symmetry of her parts is found
A power like that of harmony in sound.
Ye lofty beeches, tell this matchless dame,
That if together ye fed all one flame,
It could not equalise the hundredth part
Of what her eyes have kindled in my heart!
Go, boy, and carve this passion on the bark
Of yonder tree, which stands the sacred mark
Of noble Sidney's birth; when such benign,

Such more than mortal-making stars did shine,
That there they cannot but for ever prove
The monument and pledge of humble love;
His humble love whose hope shall ne'er rise higher,
Than for a pardon that he dares admire.

OF THE LADY WHO CAN SLEEP WHEN SHE PLEASES [1]

No wonder sleep from careful lovers flies,
To bathe himself in Saccharissa's eyes.
As fair Astraæ once from earth to heaven,
By strife and loud impiety was driven;
So with our plaints offended, and our tears,
Wise Somnus to that paradise repairs;
Waits on her will, and wretches does forsake,
To court the nymph for whom those wretches wake.
More proud than Phoebus of his throne of gold
Is the soft god those softer limbs to hold;
Nor would exchange with Jove, to hide the skies
In dark'ning clouds, the power to close her eyes;
Eyes which so far all other lights control,
They warm our mortal parts, but these our soul!
Let her free spirit, whose unconquer'd breast
Holds such deep quiet and untroubled rest,
Know that though Venus and her son should spare
Her rebel heart, and never teach her care,
Yet Hymen may in force his vigils keep,
And for another's joy suspend her sleep.

FOOTNOTE

[1] She is said to have been like Dudu—

'Large, and languishing, and lazy,
Yet of a beauty that might drive you crazy.'

OF THE MISREPORT OF HER BEING PAINTED

As when a sort of wolves infest the night
With their wild howlings at fair Cynthia's light,
The noise may chase sweet slumber from our eyes,
But never reach the mistress of the skies;
So with the news of Saccharissa's wrongs,
Her vexed servants blame those envious tongues;
Call Love to witness that no painted fire

Can scorch men so, or kindle such desire;
While, unconcern'd, she seems moved no more
With this new malice than our loves before;
But from the height of her great mind looks down
On both our passions without smile or frown.
So little care of what is done below
Hath the bright dame whom Heaven affecteth so!
Paints her, 'tis true, with the same hand which spreads
Like glorious colours through the flow'ry meads,
When lavish Nature, with her best attire,
Clothes the gay spring, the season of desire;
Paints her, 'tis true, and does her cheek adorn
With the same art wherewith she paints the morn;
With the same art wherewith she gildeth so
Those painted clouds which form Thaumantias' bow.

OF HER PASSING THROUGH A CROWD OF PEOPLE

As in old chaos (heaven with earth confused,
And stars with rocks together crush'd and bruised)
The sun his light no further could extend
Than the next hill, which on his shoulders lean'd;
So in this throng bright Saccharissa fared,
Oppress'd by those who strove to be her guard;
As ships, though never so obsequious, fall
Foul in a tempest on their admiral.
A greater favour this disorder brought
Unto her servants than their awful thought
Durst entertain, when thus compell'd they press'd
The yielding marble of her snowy breast.
While love insults,[1] disguised in the cloud,
And welcome force, of that unruly crowd.
So th'am'rous tree, while yet the air is calm,
Just distance keeps from his desired palm;[2]
But when the wind her ravish'd branches throws
Into his arms, and mingles all their boughs,
Though loth he seems her tender leaves to press,
More loth he is that friendly storm should cease,
From whose rude bounty he the double use
At once receives, of pleasure and excuse.

FOOTNOTES
[1] 'Insults': exults.
[2] 'Palm': Ovalle informs us that the palm-trees in Chili have this wonderful property, that they never will bear any fruit but when they are planted near each other; and when they find one standing barren

by itself, if they plant another, be it never so small (which they call the female), it will become prolific.—
FENTON.

THE STORY OF PHOEBUS AND DAPHNE,[1] APPLIED

Thyrsis, a youth of the inspirèd train,
Fair Saccharissa loved, but loved in vain;
Like Phoebus sung the no less am'rous boy;
Like Daphne she, as lovely, and as coy!
With numbers he the flying nymph pursues,
With numbers such as Phoebus' self might use!
Such is the chase when Love and Fancy leads,
O'er craggy mountains, and through flow'ry meads;
Invoked to testify the lover's care,
Or form some image of his cruel fair.
Urged with his fury, like a wounded deer,
O'er these he fled; and now approaching near,
Had reach'd the nymph with his harmonious lay,
Whom all his charms could not incline to stay.
Yet what he sung in his immortal strain,
Though unsuccessful, was not sung in vain;
All, but the nymph that should redress his wrong,
Attend his passion, and approve his song.
Like Phoebus thus, acquiring unsought praise,
He catch'd at love, and fill'd his arms with bays.[1]

FOOTNOTE
[1] 'Daphne': Ovid's Metamorphoses, b. i.

ON THE FRIENDSHIP BETWIXT SACCHARISSA AND AMORET

I
Tell me, lovely, loving pair!
Why so kind, and so severe?
Why so careless of our care,
Only to yourselves so dear?

II
By this cunning change of hearts,
You the power of Love control;
While the boy's deluded darts
Can arrive at neither soul.

III

For in vain to either breast
Still beguilèd Love does come,
Where he finds a foreign guest,
Neither of your hearts at home.

IV
Debtors thus with like design,
When they never mean to pay,
That they may the law decline,
To some friend make all away.

V
Not the silver doves that fly,
Yoked in Cytherea's car;
Not the wings that lift so high,
And convey her son so far;

VI
Are so lovely, sweet, and fair,
Or do more ennoble love;
Are so choicely match'd a pair,
Or with more consent do move.

AT PENSHURST [1]

While in this park I sing, the list'ning deer
Attend my passion, and forget to fear;
When to the beeches I report my flame,
They bow their heads, as if they felt the same.
To gods appealing, when I reach their bowers
With loud complaints, they answer me in showers.
To thee a wild and cruel soul is given,
More deaf than trees, and prouder than the heaven!
Love's foe profess'd! why dost thou falsely feign
Thyself a Sidney? from which noble strain
He sprung,[2] that could so far exalt the name
Of love, and warm our nation with his flame;
That all we can of love, or high desire,
Seems but the smoke of am'rous Sidney's fire.
Nor call her mother, who so well does prove
One breast may hold both chastity and love.
Never can she, that so exceeds the spring
In joy and bounty, be supposed to bring
One so destructive. To no human stock
We owe this fierce unkindness, but the rock,
That cloven rock produced thee, by whose side

Nature, to recompense the fatal pride
Of such stern beauty, placed those healing springs,[3]
Which not more help, than that destruction, brings.
Thy heart no ruder than the rugged stone,
I might, like Orpheus, with my num'rous moan
Melt to compassion; now, my trait'rous song
With thee conspires to do the singer wrong;
While thus I suffer not myself to lose
The memory of what augments my woes;
But with my own breath still foment the fire,
Which flames as high as fancy can aspire!

This last complaint th'indulgent ears did pierce
Of just Apollo, president of verse;
Highly concerned that the Muse should bring
Damage to one whom he had taught to sing,
Thus he advised me: 'On yon aged tree
Hang up thy lute, and hie thee to the sea,
That there with wonders thy diverted mind
Some truce, at least, may with this passion find.'
Ah, cruel nymph! from whom her humble swain
Flies for relief unto the raging main,
And from the winds and tempests does expect
A milder fate than from her cold neglect!
Yet there he'll pray that the unkind may prove
Bless'd in her choice; and vows this endless love
Springs from no hope of what she can confer,
But from those gifts which Heaven has heap'd on her.

FOOTNOTES
[1] 'Penshurst': his farewell verses to Dorothy.
[2] 'Sprung': Sir Philip Sidney.
[3] 'Springs': Tunbridge Wells.

THE BATTLE OF THE SUMMER ISLANDS [1]

CANTO I

What fruits they have, and how Heaven smiles
Upon these late-discovered isles.

Aid me, Bellona! while the dreadful fight
Betwixt a nation and two whales I write.
Seas stain'd with gore I sing, advent'rous toil!
And how these monsters did disarm an isle.

Bermuda, wall'd with rocks, who does not know?
That happy island where huge lemons grow,
And orange-trees, which golden fruit do bear,
Th' Hesperian garden boasts of none so fair;
Where shining pearl, coral, and many a pound,
On the rich shore, of ambergris is found.
The lofty cedar, which to heaven aspires,
The prince of trees! is fuel to their fires;
The smoke by which their loaded spits do turn,
For incense might on sacred altars burn;
Their private roofs on od'rous timber borne,
Such as might palaces for kings adorn.
The sweet palmettos a new Bacchus yield,[2]
With leaves as ample as the broadest shield,
Under the shadow of whose friendly boughs
They sit, carousing where their liquor grows.
Figs there unplanted through the fields do grow,
Such as fierce Cato did the Romans show,
With the rare fruit inviting them to spoil
Carthage, the mistress of so rich a soil.
The naked rocks are not unfruitful there,
But, at some constant seasons, every year,
Their barren tops with luscious food abound,
And with the eggs of various fowls are crown'd.
Tobacco is the worst of things, which they
To English landlords, as their tribute, pay.
Such is the mould, that the bless'd tenant feeds
On precious fruits, and pays his rent in weeds.
With candied plantains, and the juicy pine,
On choicest melons, and sweet grapes, they dine,
And with potatoes fat their wanton swine.
Nature these cates with such a lavish hand
Pours out among them, that our coarser land
Tastes of that bounty, and does cloth return,
Which not for warmth, but ornament, is worn;
For the kind spring, which but salutes us here,
Inhabits there, and courts them all the year.
Ripe fruits and blossoms on the same trees live;
At once they promise what at once they give.
So sweet the air, so moderate the clime,
None sickly lives, or dies before his time.
Heaven sure has kept this spot of earth uncursed,
To show how all things were created first.
The tardy plants in our cold orchards placed,
Reserve their fruit for the next age's taste;
There a small grain in some few months will be
A firm, a lofty, and a spacious tree.
The palma-christi, and the fair papà,

Now but a seed (preventing nature's law),
In half the circle of the hasty year
Project a shade, and lovely fruits do wear.
And as their trees in our dull region set,
But faintly grow, and no perfection get,
So, in this northern tract, our hoarser throats
Utter unripe and ill-constrained notes,
While the supporter of the poets' style,
Phoebus, on them eternally does smile.
Oh! how I long my careless limbs to lay
Under the plantain's shade, and all the day
With am'rous airs my fancy entertain,
Invoke the Muses, and improve my vein!
No passion there in my free breast should move,
None but the sweet and best of passions, love.

There while I sing, if gentle love be by,
That tunes my lute, and winds the string so high,
With the sweet sound of Saccharissa's name
I'll make the list'ning savages grow tame.—
But while I do these pleasing dreams indite,
I am diverted from the promised fight.

FOOTNOTES

[1] 'Summer Islands': the Bermudas, which received the name of the Summer Islands, or more properly, Somers' Islands, from Sir George Somers, who was cast away on the coast early in the seventeenth century, and established a colony there.

[2] 'Bacchus yield': from the palmetto, a species of palm in the West Indies, is extracted an intoxicating drink.

CANTO II

Of their alarm, and how their foes
Discover'd were, this Canto shows.

Though rocks so high about this island rise,
That well they may the num'rous Turk despise,
Yet is no human fate exempt from fear,
Which shakes their hearts, while through the isle they hear
A lasting noise, as horrid and as loud
As thunder makes before it breaks the cloud.
Three days they dread this murmur, ere they know
From what blind cause th'unwonted sound may grow.
At length two monsters of unequal size,
Hard by the shore, a fisherman espies;

Two mighty whales! which swelling seas had toss'd,
And left them pris'ners on the rocky coast.
One as a mountain vast, and with her came
A cub, not much inferior to his dam.
Here in a pool, among the rocks engaged,
They roar'd like lions caught in toils, and raged.
The man knew what they were, who heretofore
Had seen the like lie murder'd on the shore;
By the wild fury of some tempest cast,
The fate of ships, and shipwreck'd men, to taste.
As careless dames, whom wine and sleep betray
To frantic dreams, their infants overlay:
So there, sometimes, the raging ocean fails,
And her own brood exposes; when the whales
Against sharp rocks, like reeling vessels quash'd,
Though huge as mountains, are in pieces dash'd;
Along the shore their dreadful limbs lie scatter'd,
Like hills with earthquakes shaken, torn, and shatter'd.
Hearts, sure, of brass they had, who tempted first
Rude seas that spare not what themselves have nursed.
The welcome news through all the nation spread,
To sudden joy and hope converts their dread;
What lately was their public terror, they
Behold with glad eyes as a certain prey;
Dispose already of th'untaken spoil,
And as the purchase of their future toil,
These share the bones, and they divide the oil.
So was the huntsman by the bear oppress'd,
Whose hide he sold—before he caught the beast!

They man their boats, and all their young men arm
With whatsoever may the monsters harm;
Pikes, halberts, spits, and darts that wound so far,
The tools of peace, and instruments of war.
Now was the time for vig'rous lads to show
What love, or honour, could incite them to;
A goodly theatre! where rocks are round
With rev'rend age, and lovely lasses, crown'd.
Such was the lake which held this dreadful pair,
Within the bounds of noble Warwick's share:[1]
Warwick's bold Earl! than which no title bears
A greater sound among our British peers;
And worthy he the memory to renew,
The fate and honour to that title due,
Whose brave adventures have transferr'd his name,
And through the new world spread his growing fame.—

But how they fought, and what their valour gain'd,

Shall in another Canto be contain'd.

FOOTNOTE
[1] 'Warwick's share': Robert Rich, Earl of Warwick, possessed a portion of the Bermudas, which bore his name. He was a jolly sailor in his habits, although a Puritan in his profession.

CANTO III

The bloody fight, successless toil,
And how the fishes sack'd the isle.

The boat which, on the first assault did go,
Struck with a harping-iron the younger foe;
Who, when he felt his side so rudely gored,
Loud as the sea that nourished him he roar'd.
As a broad bream, to please some curious taste,
While yet alive, in boiling water cast,
Vex'd with unwonted heat he flings about
The scorching brass, and hurls the liquor out;
So with the barbed jav'lin stung, he raves,
And scourges with his tail the suffering waves.
Like Spenser's Talus with his iron flail,
He threatens ruin with his pond'rous tail;
Dissolving at one stroke the batter'd boat,
And down the men fall drenched in the moat;
With every fierce encounter they are forced
To quit their boats, and fare like men unhorsed.

The bigger whale like some huge carrack lay,
Which wanteth sea-room with her foes to play;
Slowly she swims; and when, provoked, she would
Advance her tail, her head salutes the mud;
The shallow water doth her force infringe,
And renders vain her tail's impetuous swinge;
The shining steel her tender sides receive,
And there, like bees, they all their weapons leave.

This sees the cub, and does himself oppose
Betwixt his cumber'd mother and her foes;
With desp'rate courage he receives her wounds,
And men and boats his active tail confounds.
Their forces join'd, the seas with billows fill,
And make a tempest, though the winds be still.
Now would the men with half their hopèd prey
Be well content, and wish this cub away;
Their wish they have: he (to direct his dam

Unto the gap through which they thither came)
Before her swims, and quits the hostile lake,
A pris'ner there but for his mother's sake.
She, by the rocks compell'd to stay behind,
Is by the vastness of her bulk confined.
They shout for joy! and now on her alone
Their fury falls, and all their darts are thrown.
Their lances spent, one, bolder than the rest,
With his broad sword provoked the sluggish beast;
Her oily side devours both blade and haft,
And there his steel the bold Bermudan left.
Courage the rest from his example take,
And now they change the colour of the lake;
Blood flows in rivers from her wounded side,
As if they would prevent the tardy tide,
And raise the flood to that propitious height,
As might convey her from this fatal strait.
She swims in blood, and blood does spouting throw
To heaven, that heaven men's cruelties might know.
Their fixed jav'lins in her side she wears,
And on her back a grove of pikes appears;
You would have thought, had you the monster seen
Thus dress'd, she had another island been:
Roaring she tears the air with such a noise,
As well resembled the conspiring voice
Of routed armies, when the field is won,
To reach the ears of her escapèd son.
He, though a league removèd from the foe,
Hastes to her aid; the pious Trojan[1] so,
Neglecting for Creusa's life his own,
Repeats the danger of the burning town.
The men, amazèd, blush to see the seed
Of monsters human piety exceed.
Well proves this kindness, what the Grecian sung,
That love's bright mother from the ocean sprung.
Their courage droops, and hopeless now, they wish
For composition with th'unconquered fish;
So she their weapons would restore again,
Through rocks they'd hew her passage to the main.
But how instructed in each other's mind?
Or what commerce can men with monsters find?
Not daring to approach their wounded foe,
Whom her courageous son protected so,
They charge their muskets, and, with hot desire
Of fell revenge, renew the fight with fire;
Standing aloof, with lead they bruise the scales,
And tear the flesh of the incensèd whales.
But no success their fierce endeavours found,

Nor this way could they give one fatal wound.
Now to their fort they are about to send
For the loud engines which their isle defend;
But what those pieces framed to batter walls,
Would have effected on those mighty whales,
Great Neptune will not have us know, who sends
A tide so high that it relieves his friends.
And thus they parted with exchange of harms;
Much blood the monsters lost, and they their arms.

FOOTNOTE

[1] 'Trojan': Aeneas.

OF THE QUEEN

The lark, that shuns on lofty boughs to build
Her humble nest, lies silent in the field;
But if (the promise of a cloudless day)
Aurora smiling bids her rise and play,
Then straight she shows 'twas not for want of voice,
Or power to climb, she made so low a choice;
Singing she mounts; her airy wings are stretch'd
T'wards heaven, as if from heaven her note she fetch'd.

So we, retiring from the busy throng,
Use to restrain the ambition of our song;
But since the light which now informs our age
Breaks from the Court, indulgent to her rage,
Thither my Muse, like bold Prometheus, flies,
To light her torch at Gloriana's eyes;
Those sov'reign beams which heal the wounded soul,
And all our cares, but once beheld, control!
There the poor lover that has long endured
Some proud nymph's scorn, of his fond passion cured,
Fares like the man who first upon the ground
A glow-worm spied, supposing he had found
A moving diamond, a breathing stone;
For life it had, and like those jewels shone;
He held it dear, till by the springing day
Inform'd, he threw the worthless worm away.

She saves the lover as we gangrenes stay,
By cutting hope, like a lopp'd limb, away;
This makes her bleeding patients to accuse
High Heaven, and these expostulations use:
'Could Nature then no private woman grace,

Whom we might dare to love, with such a face,
Such a complexion, and so radiant eyes,
Such lovely motion, and such sharp replies?
Beyond our reach, and yet within our sight,
What envious power has placed this glorious light?'

Thus, in a starry night, fond children cry
For the rich spangles that adorn the sky,
Which, though they shine for ever fixed there,
With light and influence relieve us here.
All her affections are to one inclined;
Her bounty and compassion to mankind;
To whom, while she so far extends her grace,
She makes but good the promise of her face;
For Mercy has, could Mercy's self be seen,
No sweeter look than this propitious queen.
Such guard, and comfort, the distressed find
From her large power, and from her larger mind,
That whom ill Fate would ruin, it prefers,
For all the miserable are made hers.
So the fair tree whereon the eagle builds,
Poor sheep from tempests, and their shepherds, shields;
The royal bird possesses all the boughs,
But shade and shelter to the flock allows.

Joy of our age, and safety of the next!
For which so oft thy fertile womb is vex'd;
Nobly contented, for the public good,
To waste thy spirits and diffuse thy blood,
What vast hopes may these islands entertain,
Where monarchs, thus descended, are to reign?
Led by commanders of so fair a line,
Our seas no longer shall our power confine.

A brave romance who would exactly frame,
First brings his knight from some immortal dame,
And then a weapon, and a flaming shield,
Bright as his mother's eyes, he makes him wield.
None might the mother of Achilles be,
But the fair pearl and glory of the sea;[1]
The man to whom great Maro gives such fame,[2]
From the high bed of heavenly Venus came;
And our next Charles, whom all the stars design
Like wonders to accomplish, springs from thine.

FOOTNOTES
[1] *'Sea': Thetis*
[2] *'Maro': Aeneas*

THE APOLOGY OF SLEEP, FOR NOT APPROACHING THE LADY WHO CAN DO ANYTHING BUT SLEEP
WHEN SHE PLEASES

My charge it is those breaches to repair
Which Nature takes from sorrow, toil, and care;
Rest to the limbs, and quiet I confer
On troubled minds; but nought can add to her
Whom Heaven, and her transcendent thoughts have placed
Above those ills which wretched mortals taste.

Bright as the deathless gods, and happy, she
From all that may infringe delight is free;
Love at her royal feet his quiver lays,
And not his mother with more haste obeys.
Such real pleasures, such true joys' suspense,
What dream can I present to recompense?

Should I with lightning fill her awful hand,
And make the clouds seem all at her command;
Or place her in Olympus' top, a guest
Among the immortals, who with nectar feast;
That power would seem, that entertainment, short
Of the true splendour of her present Court,

Where all the joys, and all the glories, are
Of three great kingdoms, sever'd from the care.
I, that of fumes and humid vapours made,
Ascending, do the seat of sense invade,
No cloud in so serene a mansion find,
To overcast her ever-shining mind,

Which holds resemblance with those spotless skies,
Where flowing Nilus want of rain supplies;
That crystal heaven, where Phoebus never shrouds
His golden beams, nor wraps his face in clouds.
But what so hard which numbers cannot force?
So stoops the moon, and rivers change their course.

The bold Mæonian[1] made me dare to steep
Jove's dreadful temples in the dew of sleep;
And since the Muses do invoke my power,
I shall no more decline that sacred bower
Where Gloriana their great mistress lies;
But, gently taming those victorious eyes,

Charm all her senses, till the joyful sun
Without a rival half his course has run;
Who, while my hand that fairer light confines,
May boast himself the brightest thing that shines.

FOOTNOTE

[1] 'Mæonian': Homer.

PUERPERIUM [1]

I
You gods that have the power
To trouble and compose
All that's beneath your bower,
Calm silence on the seas, on earth impose.

II
Fair Venus! in thy soft arms
The God of Rage confine;
For thy whispers are the charms
Which only can divert his fierce design.

III
What though he frown, and to tumult do incline?
Thou the flame
Kindled in his breast canst tame,
With that snow which unmelted lies on thine.

IV
Great goddess! give this thy sacred island rest;
Make heaven smile,
That no storm disturb us while
Thy chief care, our halcyon, builds her nest.

V
Great Gloriana! fair Gloriana!
Bright as high heaven is, and fertile as earth,
Whose beauty relieves us,
Whose royal bed gives us
Both glory and peace,
Our present joy, and all our hopes' increase.

FOOTNOTE

[1] 'Puerperium ': Fenton conjectures that this poem was written in 1640, when the Queen was delivered of her fourth son, the Duke of Gloucester.

A LA MALADE

Ah, lovely Amoret! the care
Of all that know what's good or fair!
Is heaven become our rival too?
Had the rich gifts conferr'd on you
So amply thence, the common end
Of giving lovers—to pretend?
Hence, to this pining sickness (meant
To weary thee to a consent
Of leaving us) no power is given
Thy beauties to impair; for heaven
Solicits thee with such a care,
As roses from their stalks we tear,
When we would still preserve them new
And fresh, as on the bush they grew.

With such a grace you entertain,
And look with such contempt on pain,
That languishing you conquer more,
And wound us deeper than before.
So lightnings which in storms appear,
Scorch more than when the skies are clear.

And as pale sickness does invade
Your frailer part, the breaches made
In that fair lodging, still more clear
Make the bright guest, your soul, appear.
So nymphs o'er pathless mountains borne,
Their light robes by the brambles torn
From their fair limbs, exposing new
And unknown beauties to the view
Of following gods, increase their flame
And haste to catch the flying game.

UPON THE DEATH OF MY LADY RICH [1]

May those already cursed Essexian plains,
Where hasty death and pining sickness reigns,
Prove all a desert! and none there make stay,
But savage beasts, or men as wild as they!
There the fair light which all our island graced,
Like Hero's taper in the window placed,
Such fate from the malignant air did find,

As that exposed to the boist'rous wind.

Ah, cruel Heaven! to snatch so soon away
Her for whose life, had we had time to pray,
With thousand vows and tears we should have sought
That sad decree's suspension to have wrought.
But we, alas! no whisper of her pain
Heard, till 'twas sin to wish her here again.
That horrid word, at once, like lightning spread,
Struck all our ears—The Lady Rich is dead!
Heart-rending news! and dreadful to those few
Who her resemble, and her steps pursue;
That death should license have to rage among
The fair, the wise, the virtuous, and the young!

The Paphian queen from that fierce battle borne,
With gored hand, and veil so rudely torn,
Like terror did among th'immortals breed,
Taught by her wound that goddesses may bleed.

All stand amazed! but beyond the rest
th'heroic dame whose happy womb she bless'd,[2]
Moved with just grief, expostulates with Heaven,
Urging the promise to th'obsequious given,
Of longer life; for ne'er was pious soul
More apt t'obey, more worthy to control.
A skilful eye at once might read the race
Of Caledonian monarchs in her face,
And sweet humility; her look and mind
At once were lofty, and at once were kind.
There dwelt the scorn of vice, and pity too,
For those that did what she disdain'd to do;
So gentle and severe, that what was bad,
At once her hatred and her pardon had.

Gracious to all; but where her love was due,
So fast, so faithful, loyal, and so true,
That a bold hand as soon might hope to force
The rolling lights of heaven, as change her course.

Some happy angel, that beholds her there,
Instruct us to record what she was here!
And when this cloud of sorrow's overblown,
Through the wide world we'll make her graces known.
So fresh the wound is, and the grief so vast,
That all our art and power of speech is waste.
Here passion sways, but there the Muse shall raise
Eternal monuments of louder praise.

There our delight, complying with her fame,
Shall have occasion to recite thy name,
Fair Saccharissa!—and now only fair!
To sacred friendship we'll an altar rear
(Such as the Romans did erect of old),
Where, on a marble pillar, shall be told
The lovely passion each to other bare,
With the resemblance of that matchless pair.
Narcissus to the thing for which he pined
Was not more like than yours to her fair mind,
Save that she graced the several parts of life,
A spotless virgin, and a faultless wife.
Such was the sweet converse 'twixt her and you,
As that she holds with her associates now.

How false is hope, and how regardless fate,
That such a love should have so short a date!
Lately I saw her, sighing, part from thee;
(Alas that that the last farewell should be!)
So looked Astræa, her remove design'd,
On those distressed friends she left behind.
Consent in virtue knit your hearts so fast,
That still the knot, in spite of death, does last;
For as your tears, and sorrow-wounded soul,
Prove well that on your part this bond is whole,
So all we know of what they do above,
Is that they happy are, and that they love.
Let dark oblivion, and the hollow grave,
Content themselves our frailer thoughts to have;
Well-chosen love is never taught to die,
But with our nobler part invades the sky.
Then grieve no more that one so heavenly shaped
The crooked hand of trembling age escaped;
Rather, since we beheld her not decay,
But that she vanish'd so entire away,
Her wondrous beauty, and her goodness, merit
We should suppose that some propitious spirit
In that celestial form frequented here,
And is not dead, but ceases to appear.

FOOTNOTES

[1] 'Lady Rich': she was the daughter of the Earl of Devonshire, and married to the heir of the Earl of Warwick.
[2] 'Womb she blessed': the Countess of Devonshire, a very old woman, the only daughter of Lord Bruce, descended from Robert the Bruce.

OF LOVE

Anger, in hasty words or blows,
Itself discharges on our foes;
And sorrow, too, finds some relief
In tears, which wait upon our grief;
So every passion, but fond love,
Unto its own redress does move;
But that alone the wretch inclines
To what prevents his own designs;
Makes him lament, and sigh, and weep,
Disorder'd, tremble, fawn, and creep;
Postures which render him despised,
Where he endeavours to be prized.

For women (born to be controll'd)
Stoop to the forward and the bold;
Affect the haughty and the proud,
The gay, the frolic, and the loud.
Who first the gen'rous steed oppress'd,
Not kneeling did salute the beast;
But with high courage, life, and force,
Approaching, tamed th'unruly horse.

Unwisely we the wiser East
Pity, supposing them oppress'd
With tyrants' force, whose law is will,
By which they govern, spoil and kill:
Each nymph, but moderately fair,
Commands with no less rigour here.
Should some brave Turk, that walks among
His twenty lasses, bright and young,
And beckons to the willing dame,
Preferr'd to quench his present flame,
Behold as many gallants here,
With modest guise and silent fear,
All to one female idol bend,
While her high pride does scarce descend
To mark their follies, he would swear
That these her guard of eunuchs were,
And that a more majestic queen,
Or humbler slaves, he had not seen.

All this with indignation spoke,
In vain I struggled with the yoke
Of mighty Love; that conqu'ring look,
When next beheld, like lightning strook

My blasted soul, and made me bow
Lower than those I pitied now.

So the tall stag, upon the brink
Of some smooth stream about to drink,
Surveying there his armed head,
With shame remembers that he fled
The scorned dogs, resolves to try
The combat next; but if their cry
Invades again his trembling ear,
He straight resumes his wonted care,
Leaves the untasted spring behind,
And, wing'd with fear, outflies the wind.

FOR DRINKING OF HEALTHS

Let brutes and vegetals, that cannot think,
So far as drought and nature urges, drink;
A more indulgent mistress guides our sp'rits,
Reason, that dares beyond our appetites;
(She would our care, as well as thirst, redress),
And with divinity rewards excess.
Deserted Ariadne, thus supplied,
Did perjured Theseus' cruelty deride;
Bacchus embraced, from her exalted thought
Banish'd the man, her passion, and his fault.
Bacchus and Phoebus are by Jove allied,
And each by other's timely heat supplied;
All that the grapes owe to his rip'ning fires
Is paid in numbers which their juice inspires.
Wine fills the veins, and healths are understood
To give our friends a title to our blood;
Who, naming me, doth warm his courage so,
Shows for my sake what his bold hand would do.

OF MY LADY ISABELLA, PLAYING ON THE LUTE

Such moving sounds from such a careless touch!
So unconcern'd herself, and we so much!
What art is this, that with so little pains
Transports us thus, and o'er our spirits reigns?
The trembling strings about her fingers crowd,
And tell their joy for every kiss aloud.
Small force there needs to make them tremble so;

Touch'd by that hand, who would not tremble too?
Here Love takes stand, and while she charms the ear,
Empties his quiver on the list'ning deer.
Music so softens and disarms the mind,
That not an arrow does resistance find.
Thus the fair tyrant celebrates the prize,
And acts herself the triumph of her eyes:
So Nero once, with harp in hand, survey'd
His flaming Rome, and as it burn'd he play'd.

OF MRS ARDEN [1]

Behold, and listen, while the fair
Breaks in sweet sounds the willing air,
And with her own breath fans the fire
Which her bright eyes do first inspire.
What reason can that love control,
Which more than one way courts the soul?

So when a flash of lightning falls
On our abodes, the danger calls
For human aid, which hopes the flame
To conquer, though from heaven it came;
But if the winds with that conspire,
Men strive not, but deplore the fire.

FOOTNOTE
[1] 'Mrs. Arden': some suggest that this lady was probably either a maid of honour, or a gentlewoman of
the bed-chamber to King Charles the First's Queen.

OF THE MARRIAGE OF THE DWARFS [1]

Design, or chance, makes others wive;
But Nature did this match contrive;
Eve might as well have Adam fled,
As she denied her little bed
To him, for whom Heaven seemed to frame,
And measure out, this only dame.

Thrice happy is that humble pair,
Beneath the level of all care!
Over whose heads those arrows fly
Of sad distrust and jealousy;
Secured in as high extreme,

As if the world held none but them.

To him the fairest nymphs do show
Like moving mountains, topp'd with snow;
And every man a Polypheme
Does to his Galatea seem;
None may presume her faith to prove;
He proffers death that proffers love.

Ah, Chloris! that kind Nature thus
From all the world had severed us;
Creating for ourselves us two,
As love has me for only you!

FOOTNOTE
[1] 'Dwarfs': Gibson and Shepherd, each three feet ten inches in height. They were pages at Court, and
Charles I. gave away the female infinitesimal.

LOVE'S FAREWELL

I
Treading the path to nobler ends,
A long farewell to love I gave,
Resolved my country, and my friends,
All that remain'd of me should have.

II
And this resolve no mortal dame,
None but those eyes could have o'erthrown;
The nymph I dare not, need not name,
So high, so like herself alone.

III
Thus the tall oak, which now aspires
Above the fear of private fires,
Grown and design'd for nobler use,
Not to make warm, but build the house,
Though from our meaner flames secure,
Must that which falls from heaven endure.

FROM A CHILD

Madam, as in some climes the warmer sun
Makes it full summer ere the spring's begun,

And with ripe fruit the bending boughs can load,
Before our violets dare look abroad;
So measure not by any common use
The early love your brighter eyes produce.
When lately your fair hand in woman's weed
Wrapp'd my glad head, I wish'd me so indeed,
That hasty time might never make me grow
Out of those favours you afford me now;
That I might ever such indulgence find,
And you not blush, nor think yourself too kind;
Who now, I fear, while I these joys express,
Begin to think how you may make them less.
The sound of love makes your soft heart afraid,
And guard itself, though but a child invade,
And innocently at your white breast throw
A dart as white-a ball of new fallen snow.

ON A GIRDLE

That which her slender waist confined,
Shall now my joyful temples bind;
No monarch but would give his crown,
His arms might do what this has done.

It was my heaven's extremest sphere,
The pale which held that lovely deer.
My joy, my grief, my hope, my love,
Did all within this circle move!

A narrow compass! and yet there
Dwelt all that's good, and all that's fair;
Give me but what this ribband bound,
Take all the rest the sun goes round.

THE FALL

See! how the willing earth gave way,
To take th'impression where she lay.
See! how the mould, as both to leave
So sweet a burden, still doth cleave
Close to the nymph's stain'd garment. Here
The coming spring would first appear,
And all this place with roses strow,
If busy feet would let them grow.

Here Venus smiled to see blind chance
Itself before her son advance,
And a fair image to present,
Of what the boy so long had meant.
'Twas such a chance as this, made all
The world into this order fall;
Thus the first lovers, on the clay,
Of which they were composéd, lay;
So in their prime, with equal grace,
Met the first patterns of our race.
Then blush not, fair! or on him frown,
Or wonder how you both came down;
But touch him, and he'll tremble straight,
How could he then support your weight?
How could the youth, alas! but bend,
When his whole heaven upon him lean'd?
If aught by him amiss were done,
'Twas that he let you rise so soon.

OF SYLVIA

I

Our sighs are heard; just Heaven declares
The sense it has of lovers' cares;
She that so far the rest outshined,
Sylvia the fair, while she was kind,
As if her frowns impair'd her brow,
Seems only not unhandsome now.
So, when the sky makes us endure
A storm, itself becomes obscure.

II

Hence 'tis that I conceal my flame,
Hiding from Flavia's self her name,
Lest she, provoking Heaven, should prove
How it rewards neglected love.
Better a thousand such as I,
Their grief untold, should pine and die;
Than her bright morning, overcast
With sullen clouds, should be defaced.

THE BUD

I

Lately on yonder swelling bush,
Big with many a coming rose,
This early bud began to blush,
And did but half itself disclose;
I pluck'd it, though no better grown,
And now you see how full 'tis blown.

II

Still as I did the leaves inspire,
With such a purple light they shone,
As if they had been made of fire,
And spreading so, would flame anon.
All that was meant by air or sun,
To the young flower, my breath has done.

III

If our loose breath so much can do,
What may the same in forms of love,
Of purest love, and music too,
When Flavia it aspires to move?
When that, which lifeless buds persuades
To wax more soft, her youth invades?

ON THE DISCOVERY OF A LADY'S PAINTING

I

Pygmalion's fate reversed is mine;[1]
His marble love took flesh and blood;
All that I worshipp'd as divine,
That beauty! now 'tis understood,
Appears to have no more of life
Than that whereof he framed his wife.

II

As women yet, who apprehend
Some sudden cause of causeless fear,
Although that seeming cause take end,
And they behold no danger near,
A shaking through their limbs they find,
Like leaves saluted by the wind:

III

So though the beauty do appear
No beauty, which amazed me so;
Yet from my breast I cannot tear
The passion which from thence did grow;

Nor yet out of my fancy raze
The print of that supposèd face.

IV
A real beauty, though too near,
The fond Narcissus did admire:
I dote on that which is nowhere;
The sign of beauty feeds my fire.
No mortal flame was e'er so cruel
As this, which thus survives the fuel!

FOOTNOTE
[1] 'Mine': Ovid, Met. x.

OF LOVING AT FIRST SIGHT

I
Not caring to observe the wind,
Or the new sea explore,
Snatch'd from myself, how far behind
Already I behold the shore!

II
May not a thousand dangers sleep
In the smooth bosom of this deep?
No; 'tis so reckless and so clear,
That the rich bottom does appear
Paved all with precious things; not torn
From shipwreck'd vessels, but there born.

III
Sweetness, truth, and every grace
Which time and use are wont to teach,
The eye may in a moment reach,
And read distinctly in her face.

IV
Some other nymphs, with colours faint,
And pencil slow, may Cupid paint,
And a weak heart in time destroy;
She has a stamp, and prints the boy:
Can, with a single look, inflame
The coldest breast, the rudest tame.

THE SELF-BANISHED

I
It is not that I love you less,
Than when before your feet I lay;
But to prevent the sad increase
Of hopeless love, I keep away.

II
In vain, alas! for everything
Which I have known belong to you,
Your form does to my fancy bring,
And makes my old wounds bleed anew.

III
Who in the spring, from the new sun,
Already has a fever got,
Too late begins those shafts to shun,
Which Phoebus through his veins has shot;

IV
Too late he would the pain assuage,
And to thick shadows does retire;
About with him he bears the rage,
And in his tainted blood the fire.

V
But vow'd I have, and never must
Your banish'd servant trouble you;
For if I break, you may mistrust
The vow I made—to love you too.

A PANEGYRIC TO MY LORD PROTECTOR, OF THE PRESENT GREATNESS, AND JOINT INTEREST, OF HIS HIGHNESS, AND THIS NATION [1]

I
While with a strong and yet a gentle hand,
You bridle faction, and our hearts command,
Protect us from ourselves, and from the foe,
Make us unite, and make us conquer too;

II
Let partial spirits still aloud complain,
Think themselves injured that they cannot reign,
And own no liberty but where they may
Without control upon their fellows prey.

III

Above the waves as Neptune show'd his face,
To chide the winds, and save the Trojan race,
So has your Highness, raised above the rest,
Storms of ambition, tossing us, repress'd.

IV

Your drooping country, torn with civil hate,
Restored by you, is made a glorious state;
The seat of empire, where the Irish come,
And the unwilling Scots, to fetch their doom.

V

The sea's our own; and now all nations greet,
With bending sails, each vessel of our fleet;
Your power extends as far as winds can blow,
Or swelling sails upon the globe may go.

VI

Heaven (that hath placed this island to give law,
To balance Europe, and her states to awe),
In this conjunction doth on Britain smile;
The greatest leader, and the greatest isle!

VII

Whether this portion of the world were rent,
By the rude ocean, from the continent,
Or thus created, it was sure design'd
To be the sacred refuge of mankind.

VIII

Hither th'oppressed shall henceforth resort,
Justice to crave, and succour, at your court;
And then your Highness, not for ours alone,
But for the world's Protector shall be known.

IX

Fame, swifter than your winged navy, flies
Through every land that near the ocean lies,
Sounding your name, and telling dreadful news
To all that piracy and rapine use.

X

With such a chief the meanest nation bless'd,
Might hope to lift her head above the rest;
What may be thought impossible to do
By us, embraced by the sea and you?

XI

Lords of the world's great waste, the ocean, we
Whole forests send to reign upon the sea,
And every coast may trouble, or relieve;
But none can visit us without your leave.

XII

Angels and we have this prerogative,
That none can at our happy seats arrive;
While we descend at pleasure, to invade
The bad with vengeance, and the good to aid.

XIII

Our little world, the image of the great,
Like that, amidst the boundless ocean set,
Of her own growth hath all that Nature craves,
And all that's rare, as tribute from the waves.

XIV

As Egypt does not on the clouds rely,
But to the Nile owes more than to the sky;
So what our earth, and what our heaven denies,
Our ever constant friend, the sea, supplies.

XV

The taste of hot Arabia's spice we know,
Free from the scorching sun that makes it grow;
Without the worm, in Persian silks we shine;
And, without planting, drink of every vine.

XVI

To dig for wealth we weary not our limbs;
Gold, though the heaviest metal, hither swims;
Ours is the harvest where the Indians mow;
We plough the deep, and reap what others sow.

XVII

Things of the noblest kind our own soil breeds;
Stout are our men, and warlike are our steeds;
Rome, though her eagle through the world had flown,
Could never make this island all her own.

XVIII

Here the Third Edward, and the Black Prince, too,
France-conqu'ring Henry flourish'd, and now you;
For whom we stay'd, as did the Grecian state,
Till Alexander came to urge their fate.

XIX

When for more worlds the Macedonian cried,
He wist not Thetis in her lap did hide
Another yet; a world reserved for you,
To make more great than that he did subdue.

XX

He safely might old troops to battle lead,
Against th'unwarlike Persian and the Mede,
Whose hasty flight did, from a bloodless field,
More spoils than honour to the victor yield.

XXI

A race unconquer'd, by their clime made bold,
The Caledonians, arm'd with want and cold,
Have, by a fate indulgent to your fame,
Been from all ages kept for you to tame.

XXII

Whom the old Roman wall so ill confined,
With a new chain of garrisons you bind;
Here foreign gold no more shall make them come;
Our English iron holds them fast at home.

XXIII

They, that henceforth must be content to know
No warmer regions than their hills of snow,
May blame the sun, but must extol your grace,
Which in our senate hath allowed them place.

XXIV

Preferr'd by conquest, happily o'erthrown,
Falling they rise, to be with us made one;
So kind Dictators made, when they came home,
Their vanquish'd foes free citizens of Rome.

XXV

Like favour find the Irish, with like fate,
Advanced to be a portion of our state;
While by your valour and your bounteous mind,
Nations, divided by the sea, are join'd.

XXVI

Holland, to gain your friendship, is content
To be our outguard on the Continent;
She from her fellow-provinces would go,
Rather than hazard to have you her foe.

XXVII

In our late fight, when cannons did diffuse,
Preventing posts, the terror and the news,
Our neighbour princes trembled at their roar;
But our conjunction makes them tremble more.

XXVIII

Your never-failing sword made war to cease;
And now you heal us with the acts of peace;
Our minds with bounty and with awe engage,
Invite affection, and restrain our rage.

XXIX

Less pleasure take brave minds in battles won,
Than in restoring such as are undone;
Tigers have courage, and the rugged bear,
But man alone can, whom he conquers, spare.

XXX

To pardon willing, and to punish loth,
You strike with one hand, but you heal with both;
Lifting up all that prostrate lie, you grieve
You cannot make the dead again to live.

XXXI

When fate, or error, had our age misled,
And o'er this nation such confusion spread,
The only cure, which could from Heaven come down,
Was so much power and piety in one!

XXXII

One! whose extraction from an ancient line
Gives hope again that well-born men may shine;
The meanest in your nature, mild and good,
The noblest rest secured in your blood.

XXXIII

Oft have we wonder'd how you hid in peace
A mind proportion'd to such things as these;
How such a ruling sp'rit you could restrain,
And practise first over yourself to reign.

XXXIV

Your private life did a just pattern give,
How fathers, husbands, pious sons should live;
Born to command, your princely virtues slept,
Like humble David's, while the flock he kept.

XXXV

But when your troubled country called you forth,
Your flaming courage, and your matchless worth,
Dazzling the eyes of all that did pretend,
To fierce contention gave a prosp'rous end.

XXXVI

Still as you rise, the state, exalted too,
Finds no distemper while 'tis changed by you;
Changed like the world's great scene! when, without noise,
The rising sun night's vulgar light destroys.

XXXVII

Had you, some ages past, this race of glory
Run, with amazement we should read your story;
But living virtue, all achievements past,
Meets envy still, to grapple with at last.

XXXVIII

This Cæsar found; and that ungrateful age,
With losing him went back to blood and rage;
Mistaken Brutus thought to break their yoke,
But cut the bond of union with that stroke.

XXXIX

That sun once set, a thousand meaner stars
Gave a dim light to violence and wars,
To such a tempest as now threatens all,
Did not your mighty arm prevent the fall.

XL

If Rome's great senate could not wield that sword,
Which of the conquer'd world had made them lord;
What hope had ours, while yet their power was new,
To rule victorious armies, but by you?

XLI

You! that had taught them to subdue their foes,
Could order teach, and their high sp'rits compose;
To every duty could their minds engage,
Provoke their courage, and command their rage.

XLII

So when a lion shakes his dreadful mane,
And angry grows, if he that first took pain
To tame his youth approach the haughty beast,
He bends to him, but frights away the rest.

XLIII

As the vex'd world, to find repose, at last
Itself into Augustus' arms did cast;
So England now does, with like toil oppress'd,
Her weary head upon your bosom rest.

XLIV

Then let the Muses, with such notes as these,
Instruct us what belongs unto our peace;
Your battles they hereafter shall indite,
And draw the image of our Mars in fight;

XLV

Tell of towns storm'd, of armies overrun,
And mighty kingdoms by your conduct won;
How, while you thunder'd, clouds of dust did choke
Contending troops, and seas lay hid in smoke.

XLVI

Illustrious acts high raptures do infuse,
And every conqueror creates a Muse.
Here, in low strains, your milder deeds we sing;
But there, my lord! we'll bays and olive bring,

XLVII

To crown your head; while you in triumph ride
O'er vanquish'd nations, and the sea beside;
While all your neighbour princes unto you,
Like Joseph's sheaves,[2] pay reverence, and bow.

FOOTNOTES
[1] Written about 1654.
[2] 'Joseph's sheaves': Gen. xxxvii.

ON THE HEAD OF A STAG

So we some antique hero's strength
Learn by his lance's weight and length,
As these vast beams express the beast
Whose shady brows alive they dress'd.
Such game, while yet the world was new,
The mighty Nimrod did pursue.
What huntsman of our feeble race,
Or dogs, dare such a monster chase,
Resembling, with each blow he strikes,

The charge of a whole troop of pikes?
O fertile head! which every year
Could such a crop of wonder bear?
The teeming earth did never bring
So soon, so hard, so huge a thing;
Which might it never have been cast
(Each year's growth added to the last),
These lofty branches had supplied
The earth's bold sons' prodigious pride;
Heaven with these engines had been scaled,
When mountains heap'd on mountains fail'd.

THE MISER'S SPEECH. IN A MASQUE

Balls of this metal slack'd At'lanta's pace,
And on the am'rous youth[1] bestow'd the race;
Venus (the nymph's mind measuring by her own),
Whom the rich spoils of cities overthrown
Had prostrated to Mars, could well advise
Th' advent'rous lover how to gain the prize.
Nor less may Jupiter to gold ascribe;
For, when he turn'd himself into a bribe,
Who can blame Danaë[2], or the brazen tower,
That they withstood not that almighty shower
Never till then did love make Jove put on
A form more bright, and nobler than his own;
Nor were it just, would he resume that shape,
That slack devotion should his thunder 'scape.
'Twas not revenge for griev'd Apollo's wrong,
Those ass's ears on Midas' temples hung,
But fond repentance of his happy wish,
Because his meat grew metal like his dish.
Would Bacchus bless me so, I'd constant hold
Unto my wish, and die creating gold.

FOOTNOTES
[1] 'Am'rous youth': Hippomenes.
[2] Transcriber's note: The original text has a single dot over the second "a" and another over the "e", rather than the more conventional diaresis shown here.

CHLORIS AND HYLAS. MADE TO A SARABAND

CHLORIS.
Hylas, O Hylas! why sit we mute,

Now that each bird saluteth the spring?
Wind up the slacken'd strings of thy lute,
Never canst thou want matter to sing;
For love thy breast does fill with such a fire,
That whatsoe'er is fair moves thy desire.

HYLAS.
Sweetest! you know, the sweetest of things
Of various flowers the bees do compose;
Yet no particular taste it brings
Of violet, woodbine, pink, or rose;
So love the result is of all the graces
Which flow from a thousand sev'ral faces.

CHLORIS.
Hylas! the birds which chant in this grove,
Could we but know the language they use,
They would instruct us better in love,
And reprehend thy inconstant Muse;
For love their breasts does fill with such a fire,
That what they once do choose, bounds their desire.

HYLAS.
Chloris! this change the birds do approve,
Which the warm season hither does bring;
Time from yourself does further remove
You, than the winter from the gay spring;
She that like lightning shined while her face lasted,
The oak now resembles which lightning hath blasted.

IN ANSWER OF SIR JOHN SUCKLING'S VERSES

CON.
Stay here, fond youth! and ask no more; be wise;
Knowing too much long since lost Paradise.

PRO.
And, by your knowledge, we should be bereft
Of all that Paradise which yet is left.

CON.
The virtuous joys thou hast, thou wouldst should still
Last in their pride; and wouldst not take it ill
If rudely from sweet dreams, and for a toy,
Thou waked; he wakes himself that does enjoy.

PRO.
How can the joy, or hope, which you allow
Be styled virtuous, and the end not so?
Talk in your sleep, and shadows still admire!
'Tis true, he wakes that feels this real fire;
But—to sleep better; for whoe'er drinks deep
Of this Nepenthe, rocks himself asleep.

CON.
Fruition adds no new wealth, but destroys,
And while it pleaseth much, yet still it cloys.
Who thinks he should be happier made for that,
As reasonably might hope he might grow fat
By eating to a surfeit; this once past,
What relishes? even kisses lose their taste.

PRO.
Blessings may be repeated while they cloy;
But shall we starve, 'cause surfeitings destroy?
And if fruition did the taste impair
Of kisses, why should yonder happy pair,
Whose joys just Hymen warrants all the night,
Consume the day, too, in this less delight?

CON.
Urge not 'tis necessary; alas! we know
The homeliest thing that mankind does is so.
The world is of a large extent we see,
And must be peopled; children there must be:
So must bread too; but since there are enow
Born to that drudgery, what need we plough?

PRO.
I need not plough, since what the stooping hine[1]
Gets of my pregnant land must all be mine;
But in this nobler tillage 'tis not so;
For when Anchises did fair Venus know,
What interest had poor Vulcan in the boy,
Famous Aeneas, or the present joy?

CON.
Women enjoy'd, whate'er before they've been,
Are like romances read, or scenes once seen;
Fruition dulls or spoils the play much more
Than if one read, or knew the plot before.

PRO.
Plays and romances read and seen, do fall

In our opinions; yet not seen at all,
Whom would they please? To an heroic tale
Would you not listen, lest it should grow stale?

CON.
'Tis expectation makes a blessing dear;
Heaven were not heaven, if we knew what it were.

PRO.
If 'twere not heaven if we knew what it were,
'Twould not be heaven to those that now are there.

CON.
And as in prospects we are there pleased most,
Where something keeps the eye from being lost,
And leaves us room to guess; so here, restraint
Holds up delight, that with excess would faint.

PRO.

Restraint preserves the pleasure we have got,
But he ne'er has it that enjoys it not.
In goodly prospects, who contracts the space,
Or takes not all the bounty of the place?
We wish remov'd what standeth in our light,
And nature blame for limiting our sight;
Where you stand wisely winking, that the view
Of the fair prospect may be always new.

CON.
They, who know all the wealth they have, are poor;
He's only rich that cannot tell his store.

PRO.
Not he that knows the wealth he has is poor,
But he that dares not touch, nor use, his store.

FOOTNOTE
[1] 'Hine': hind.

AN APOLOGY FOR HAVING LOVED BEFORE

I
They that never had the use
Of the grape's surprising juice,

To the first delicious cup
All their reason render up;
Neither do, nor care to know,
Whether it be best or no.

II

So they that are to love inclined,
Sway'd by chance, not choice or art,
To the first that's fair, or kind,
Make a present of their heart;
'Tis not she that first we love,
But whom dying we approve.

III

To man, that was in th'ev'ning made,
Stars gave the first delight,
Admiring, in the gloomy shade,
Those little drops of light;
Then at Aurora, whose fair hand
Removed them from the skies,
He gazing t'ward the east did stand,
She entertain'd his eyes.

IV

But when the bright sun did appear,
All those he 'gan despise;
His wonder was determined there,
And could no higher rise;
He neither might, nor wished to know
A more refulgent light;
For that (as mine your beauties now)
Employ'd his utmost sight.

THE NIGHT-PIECE; OR, A PICTURE DRAWN IN THE DARK

Darkness, which fairest nymphs disarms,
Defends us ill from Mira's charms;
Mira can lay her beauty by,
Take no advantage of the eye,
Quit all that Lely's art can take,
And yet a thousand captives make.

Her speech is graced with sweeter sound
Than in another's song is found!
And all her well-placed words are darts,
Which need no light to reach our hearts.

As the bright stars and Milky Way,
Show'd by the night, are hid by day;
So we, in that accomplish'd mind,
Help'd by the night, new graces find,
Which, by the splendour of her view,
Dazzled before, we never knew.

While we converse with her, we mark
No want of day, nor think it dark;
Her shining image is a light
Fix'd in our hearts, and conquers night.

Like jewels to advantage set,
Her beauty by the shade does get;
There blushes, frowns, and cold disdain,
All that our passion might restrain,
Is hid, and our indulgent mind
Presents the fair idea kind.

Yet, friended by the night, we dare
Only in whispers tell our care;
He that on her his bold hand lays,
With Cupid's pointed arrows plays;
They with a touch (they are so keen!)
Wound us unshot, and she unseen.

All near approaches threaten death;
We may be shipwreck'd by her breath;
Love, favour'd once with that sweet gale,
Doubles his haste, and fills his sail,
Till he arrive where she must prove
The haven, or the rock, of love.

So we th'Arabian coast do know
At distance, when the spices blow;
By the rich odour taught to steer,
Though neither day nor stars appear.

ON THE PICTURE OF A FAIR YOUTH, TAKEN AFTER HE WAS DEAD

As gather'd flowers, while their wounds are new,
Look gay and fresh, as on the stalk they grew;
Torn from the root that nourish'd them, awhile
(Not taking notice of their fate) they smile,
And, in the hand which rudely pluck'd them, show
Fairer than those that to their autumn grow;

So love and beauty still that visage grace;
Death cannot fright them from their wonted place.
Alive, the hand of crooked Age had marr'd,
Those lovely features which cold Death has spared.

No wonder then he sped in love so well,
When his high passion he had breath to tell;
When that accomplish'd soul, in this fair frame,
No business had but to persuade that dame,
Whose mutual love advanced the youth so high,
That, but to heaven, he could no higher fly.

ON A BREDE OF DIVERS COLOURS, WOVEN BY FOUR LADIES

Twice twenty slender virgin-fingers twine
This curious web, where all their fancies shine.
As Nature them, so they this shade have wrought,
Soft as their hands, and various as their thought;
Not Juno's bird when, his fair train dispread,
He woos the female to his painted bed,
No, not the bow, which so adorns the skies,
So glorious is, or boasts so many dyes.

OF A WAR WITH SPAIN, AND FIGHT AT SEA [1]

Now, for some ages, had the pride of Spain
Made the sun shine on half the world in vain;
While she bid war to all that durst supply
The place of those her cruelty made die.
Of Nature's bounty men forebore to taste,
And the best portion of the earth lay waste.
From the new world, her silver and her gold
Came, like a tempest, to confound the old;
Feeding with these the bribed electors' hopes,
Alone she gives us emperors and popes;
With these accomplishing her vast designs,
Europe was shaken with her Indian mines.

When Britain, looking with a just disdain
Upon this gilded majesty of Spain,
And knowing well that empire must decline,
Whose chief support and sinews are of coin,
Our nation's solid virtue did oppose
To the rich troublers of the world's repose.

And now some months, encamping on the main,
Our naval army had besiegèd Spain;
They that the whole world's monarchy design'd,
Are to their ports by our bold fleet confined;
From whence our Red Cross they triumphant see,
Riding without a rival on the sea.

Others may use the ocean as their road,
Only the English make it their abode,
Whose ready sails with every wind can fly,
And make a cov'nant with th'inconstant sky;
Our oaks secure, as if they there took root,
We tread on billows with a steady foot.

Meanwhile the Spaniards in America,
Near to the line the sun approaching saw,
And hoped their European coasts to find
Clear'd from our ships by the autumnal wind;
Their huge capacious galleons stuff'd with plate,
The lab'ring winds drive slowly t'wards their fate.
Before St. Lucar they their guns discharge
To tell their joy, or to invite a barge;
This heard some ships of ours (though out of view),
And, swift as eagles, to the quarry flew;
So heedless lambs, which for their mothers bleat,
Wake hungry lions, and become their meat.

Arrived, they soon begin that tragic play,
And with their smoky cannons banish day;
Night, horror, slaughter, with confusion meets,
And in their sable arms embrace the fleets.
Through yielding planks the angry bullets fly,
And, of one wound, hundreds together die;
Born under diff'rent stars, one fate they have,
The ship their coffin, and the sea their grave!
Bold were the men which on the ocean first
Spread their new sails, when shipwreck was the worst;
More danger now from man alone we find
Than from the rocks, the billows, or the wind.
They that had sail'd from near th'Antarctic Pole,
Their treasure safe, and all their vessels whole,
In sight of their dear country ruin'd be,
Without the guilt of either rock or sea!
What they would spare, our fiercer art destroys,
Surpassing storms in terror and in noise.
Once Jove from Ida did both hosts survey,
And, when he pleased to thunder, part the fray;

Here, heaven in vain that kind retreat should sound,
The louder cannon had the thunder drown'd.
Some we made prize; while others, burn'd and rent,
With their rich lading to the bottom went;
Down sinks at once (so Fortune with us sports:)
The pay of armies, and the pride of courts.
Vain man! whose rage buries as low that store,
As avarice had digg'd for it before;
What earth, in her dark bowels, could not keep
From greedy hands, lies safer in the deep,
Where Thetis kindly does from mortals hide
Those seeds of luxury, debate, and pride.

And now, into her lap the richest prize
Fell, with the noblest of our enemies;
The Marquis[2](glad to see the fire destroy
Wealth that prevailing foes were to enjoy)
Out from his flaming ship his children sent,
To perish in a milder element;
Then laid him by his burning lady's side,
And, since he could not save her, with her died.
Spices and gums about them melting fry,
And, phoenix-like, in that rich nest they die;
Alive, in flames of equal love they burn'd,
And now together are to ashes turn'd;
Ashes! more worth than all their fun'ral cost,
Than the huge treasure which was with them lost.
These dying lovers, and their floating sons,
Suspend the fight, and silence all our guns;
Beauty and youth about to perish, finds
Such noble pity in brave English minds,
That (the rich spoil forgot, their valour's prize,)
All labour now to save their enemies.

How frail our passions! how soon changèd are
Our wrath and fury to a friendly care!
They that but now for honour, and for plate,
Made the sea blush with blood, resign their hate;
And, their young foes endeav'ring to retrieve,
With greater hazard than they fought, they dive.

With these, returns victorious Montague,
With laurels in his hand, and half Peru.
Let the brave generals divide that bough,
Our great Protector hath such wreaths enow;
His conqu'ring head has no more room for bays;
Then let it be as the glad nation prays;

Let the rich ore forthwith be melted down,
And the state fix'd by making him a crown;
With ermine clad, and purple, let him hold
A royal sceptre, made of Spanish gold.

FOOTNOTES

[1] 'Fight at sea': see any good English History, under date 1656.
[2] 'Marquis': of Badajos, viceroy of Mexico.

UPON THE DEATH OF THE LORD PROTECTOR

We must resign! Heaven his great soul does claim
In storms, as loud as his immortal fame;
His dying groans, his last breath, shakes our isle,
And trees uncut fall for his funeral pile;
About his palace their broad roots are toss'd
Into the air.[1]—So Romulus was lost!
New Rome in such a tempest miss'd her king,
And from obeying fell to worshipping.
On Oeta's top thus Hercules lay dead,
With ruin'd oaks and pines about him spread;
The poplar, too, whose bough he wont to wear
On his victorious head, lay prostrate there;
Those his last fury from the mountain rent:
Our dying hero from the Continent
Ravish'd whole towns: and forts from Spaniards reft
As his last legacy to Britain left.
The ocean, which so long our hopes confined,
Could give no limits to his vaster mind;
Our bounds' enlargement was his latest toil,
Nor hath he left us pris'ners to our isle;
Under the tropic is our language spoke,
And part of Flanders hath received our yoke.
From civil broils he did us disengage,
Found nobler objects for our martial rage;
And, with wise conduct, to his country show'd
The ancient way of conquering abroad.
Ungrateful then! if we no tears allow
To him, that gave us peace and empire too.
Princes, that fear'd him, grieve, concern'd to see
No pitch of glory from the grave is free.
Nature herself took notice of his death,
And, sighing, swell'd the sea with such a breath,
That, to remotest shores her billows roll'd,
The approaching fate of their great ruler told.

FOOTNOTE

[1] 'The air': a tremendous tempest blew over England (not on the day), but a day or two before
Cromwell's death. It was said that something of the same sort, along with an eclipse of the sun, took
place on the removal of Romulus.

ON ST JAMES'S PARK, AS LATELY IMPROVED BY HIS MAJESTY [1]

Of the first Paradise there's nothing found;
Plants set by Heaven are vanish'd, and the ground;
Yet the description lasts; who knows the fate
Of lines that shall this paradise relate?

Instead of rivers rolling by the side
Of Eden's garden, here flows in the tide;
The sea, which always served his empire, now
Pays tribute to our Prince's pleasure too.
Of famous cities we the founders know;
But rivers, old as seas, to which they go,
Are Nature's bounty; 'tis of more renown
To make a river, than to build a town.

For future shade, young trees upon the banks
Of the new stream appear in even ranks;
The voice of Orpheus, or Amphion's hand,
In better order could not make them stand;
May they increase as fast, and spread their boughs,
As the high fame of their great owner grows!
May he live long enough to see them all
Dark shadows cast, and as his palace tall!
Methinks I see the love that shall be made,
The lovers walking in that am'rous shade;
The gallants dancing by the river side;
They bathe in summer, and in winter slide.
Methinks I hear the music in the boats,
And the loud echo which returns the notes;
While overhead a flock of new-sprung fowl
Hangs in the air, and does the sun control,
Dark'ning the sky; they hover o'er, and shroud
The wanton sailors with a feather'd cloud.
Beneath, a shoal of silver fishes glides,
And plays about the gilded barges' sides;
The ladies, angling in the crystal lake,
Feast on the waters with the prey they take;
At once victorious with their lines, and eyes,
They make the fishes, and the men, their prize.
A thousand Cupids on the billows ride,

And sea-nymphs enter with the swelling tide,
From Thetis sent as spies, to make report,
And tell the wonders of her sovereign's court.
All that can, living, feed the greedy eye,
Or dead, the palate, here you may descry;
The choicest things that furnish'd Noah's ark,
Or Peter's sheet, inhabiting this park;
All with a border of rich fruit-trees crown'd,
Whose loaded branches hide the lofty mound,
Such various ways the spacious alleys lead,
My doubtful Muse knows not what path to tread.
Yonder, the harvest of cold months laid up,
Gives a fresh coolness to the royal cup;
There ice, like crystal firm, and never lost,
Tempers hot July with December's frost;
Winter's dark prison, whence he cannot fly,
Though the warm spring, his enemy, draws nigh.
Strange! that extremes should thus preserve the snow,
High on the Alps, or in deep caves below.

Here, a well-polished Mall gives us the joy
To see our Prince his matchless force employ;
His manly posture, and his graceful mien,
Vigour and youth in all his motions seen;
His shape so lovely and his limbs so strong,
Confirm our hopes we shall obey him long.

No sooner has he touch'd the flying ball,
But 'tis already more than half the Mall;
And such a fury from his arm has got,
As from a smoking culv'rin it were shot.[2]

Near this my Muse, what most delights her, sees
A living gallery of aged trees;
Bold sons of earth, that thrust their arms so high,
As if once more they would invade the sky.
In such green palaces the first kings reign'd,
Slept in their shades, and angels entertain'd;
With such old counsellors they did advise,
And, by frequenting sacred groves, grew wise.
Free from th'impediments of light and noise,
Man, thus retired, his nobler thoughts employs.
Here Charles contrives th'ordering of his states,
Here he resolves his neighb'ring princes' fates;
What nation shall have peace, where war be made,
Determined is in this oraculous shade;
The world, from India to the frozen north,
Concern'd in what this solitude brings forth.

His fancy objects from his view receives;
The prospect thought and contemplation gives.
That seat of empire here salutes his eye,
To which three kingdoms do themselves apply;
The structure by a prelate[3] raised, Whitehall,
Built with the fortune of Rome's capitol;
Both, disproportion'd to the present state
Of their proud founders, were approved by Fate.
From hence he does that antique pile[4] behold,
Where royal heads receive the sacred gold;
It gives them crowns, and does their ashes keep;
There made like gods, like mortals there they sleep;
Making the circle of their reign complete,
Those suns of empire! where they rise, they set.
When others fell, this, standing, did presage
The crown should triumph over popular rage;
Hard by that House,[5] where all our ills were shaped,
Th' auspicious temple stood, and yet escaped.
So snow on Aetna does unmelted lie,
Whence rolling flames and scatter'd cinders fly;
The distant country in the ruin shares;
What falls from heaven the burning mountain spares.
Next, that capacious Hall[6] he sees, the room
Where the whole nation does for justice come;
Under whose large roof flourishes the gown,
And judges grave, on high tribunals, frown.
Here, like the people's pastor he does go,
His flock subjected to his view below;
On which reflecting in his mighty mind,
No private passion does indulgence find;
The pleasures of his youth suspended are,
And made a sacrifice to public care.
Here, free from court compliances, he walks,
And with himself, his best adviser, talks;
How peaceful olives may his temples shade,
For mending laws, and for restoring trade;
Or, how his brows may be with laurel charged,
For nations conquer'd and our bounds enlarged.
Of ancient prudence here he ruminates,
Of rising kingdoms, and of falling states;
What ruling arts gave great Augustus fame,
And how Alcides purchased such a name.

His eyes, upon his native palace[7] bent,
Close by, suggest a greater argument.
His thoughts rise higher, when he does reflect
On what the world may from that star expect
Which at his birth appear'd,[8] to let us see

Day, for his sake, could with the night agree;
A prince, on whom such diff'rent lights did smile,
Born the divided world to reconcile!
Whatever Heaven, or high extracted blood
Could promise, or foretell, he will make good;
Reform these nations, and improve them more,
Than this fair park, from what it was before.

FOOTNOTES

[1] See 'Macaulay.'
[2] Pall Mall derived its name from a particular game at bowls, in which Charles II. excelled.
[3] 'Prelate': Cardinal Wolsey.
[4] 'Antique pile': Westminster Abbey.
[5] 'House': House of Commons.
[6] 'Hall': Westminster Hall.
[7] 'Palace': St. James's Palace, where Charles II. was born.
[8] 'Birth appeared ': it seems a new star appeared in the heavens at the birth of the king.

OF HER ROYAL HIGHNESS, MOTHER TO THE PRINCE OF ORANGE;[1] AND OF HER PORTRAIT, WRITTEN BY THE LATE DUCHESS OF YORK, WHILE SHE LIVED WITH HER

Heroic nymph! in tempests the support,
In peace the glory of the British Court!
Into whose arms the church, the state, and all
That precious is, or sacred here, did fall.
Ages to come, that shall your bounty hear,
Will think you mistress of the Indies were;
Though straiter bounds your fortunes did confine,
In your large heart was found a wealthy mine;
Like the bless'd oil, the widow's lasting feast,
Your treasure, as you pour'd it out, increased.

While some your beauty, some your bounty sing,
Your native isle does with your praises ring;
But, above all, a nymph of your own train[2]
Gives us your character in such a strain,
As none but she, who in that Court did dwell,
Could know such worth, or worth describe so well.
So while we mortals here at heaven do guess,
And more our weakness, than the place, express,
Some angel, a domestic there, comes down,
And tells the wonders he hath seen and known.

FOOTNOTES

[1] 'Prince of Orange': Mary, Princess of Orange, and sister to Charles II.

[2] 'Train': Lady Anne Hyde, daughter of the Earl of Clarendon, and afterwards Duchess of York, and mother of Queen Mary and Queen Anne.

UPON HER MAJESTY'S NEW BUILDINGS AT SOMERSET HOUSE [1]

Great Queen! that does our island bless
With princes and with palaces;
Treated so ill, chased from your throne,
Returning you adorn the Town;
And, with a brave revenge, do show
Their glory went and came with you.

While peace from hence and you were gone,
Your houses in that storm o'erthrown,
Those wounds which civil rage did give,
At once you pardon, and relieve.

Constant to England in your love,
As birds are to their wonted grove,
Though by rude hands their nests are spoil'd,
There the next spring again they build.

Accusing some malignant star,
Not Britain, for that fatal war,
Your kindness banishes your fear,
Resolved to fix for ever here.[2]
But what new mine this work supplies?
Can such a pile from ruin rise?
This, like the first creation, shows
As if at your command it rose.

Frugality and bounty too
(Those diff'ring virtues), meet in you;
From a confined, well-managed store,
You both employ and feed the poor.

Let foreign princes vainly boast
The rude effects of pride, and cost
Of vaster fabrics, to which they
Contribute nothing but the pay;
This, by the Queen herself design'd,
Gives us a pattern of her mind;
The state and order does proclaim
The genius of that Royal Dame.
Each part with just proportion graced,
And all to such advantage placed,

That the fair view her window yields,
The town, the river, and the fields,
Ent'ring, beneath us we descry,
And wonder how we came so high.

She needs no weary steps ascend;
All seems before her feet to bend;
And here, as she was born, she lies;
High, without taking pains to rise.

FOOTNOTES

[1] 'Somerset House': Henrietta, Queen-mother, who returned to England in 1660, and lived in Somerset House, which she greatly improved.
[2] 'Ever here': she left, however, in 1665.

OF A TREE CUT IN PAPER

Fair hand! that can on virgin paper write,
Yet from the stain of ink preserve it white;
Whose travel o'er that silver field does show
Like track of leverets in morning snow.
Love's image thus in purest minds is wrought,
Without a spot or blemish to the thought.
Strange, that your fingers should the pencil foil,
Without the help of colours or of oil!
For though a painter boughs and leaves can make,
'Tis you alone can make them bend and shake;
Whose breath salutes your new-created grove,
Like southern winds, and makes it gently move.
Orpheus could make the forest dance; but you
Can make the motion and the forest too.

VERSES TO DR GEORGE ROGERS, ON HIS TAKING THE DEGREE OF DOCTOR OF PHYSIC AT PADUA, IN THE YEAR 1664

When as of old the earth's bold children strove,
With hills on hills, to scale the throne of Jove,
Pallas and Mars stood by their sovereign's side,
And their bright arms in his defence employ'd;
While the wise Phoebus, Hermes, and the rest,
Who joy in peace, and love the Muses best,
Descending from their so distemper'd seat,
Our groves and meadows chose for their retreat.
There first Apollo tried the various use

Of herbs, and learn'd the virtues of their juice,
And framed that art, to which who can pretend
A juster title than our noble friend,
Whom the like tempest drives from his abode,
And like employment entertains abroad?
This crowns him here, and in the bays so earn'd,
His country's honour is no less concern'd,
Since it appears not all the English rave,
To ruin bent; some study how to save;
And as Hippocrates did once extend
His sacred art, whole cities to amend;
So we, great friend! suppose that thy great skill,
Thy gentle mind, and fair example will,
At thy return, reclaim our frantic isle,
Their spirits calm, and peace again shall smile.

INSTRUCTIONS TO A PAINTER, FOR THE DRAWING OF THE POSTURE AND PROGRESS OF HIS MAJESTY'S FORCES AT SEA, UNDER THE COMMAND OF HIS HIGHNESS-ROYAL; TOGETHER WITH THE BATTLE AND VICTORY OBTAINED OVER THE DUTCH, JUNE 3, 1665 [1]

First draw the sea, that portion which between
The greater world and this of ours is seen;
Here place the British, there the Holland fleet,
Vast floating armies! both prepared to meet.
Draw the whole world, expecting who should reign,
After this combat, o'er the conquer'd main.

Make Heaven concern'd, and an unusual star
Declare th'importance of th'approaching war.
Make the sea shine with gallantry, and all
The English youth flock to their Admiral,
The valiant Duke! whose early deeds abroad,
Such rage in fight, and art in conduct show'd.
His bright sword now a dearer int'rest draws,
His brother's glory, and his country's cause.

Let thy bold pencil hope and courage spread,
Through the whole navy, by that hero led;
Make all appear, where such a Prince is by,
Resolved to conquer, or resolved to die.
With his extraction, and his glorious mind,
Make the proud sails swell more than with the wind;
Preventing cannon, make his louder fame
Check the Batavians, and their fury tame.
So hungry wolves, though greedy of their prey,
Stop when they find a lion in their way.

Make him bestride the ocean, and mankind
Ask his consent to use the sea and wind;
While his tall ships in the barr'd channel stand,
He grasps the Indies in his armed hand.

Paint an east wind, and make it blow away
Th' excuse of Holland for their navy's stay;
Make them look pale, and, the bold Prince to shun,
Through the cold north and rocky regions run.
To find the coast where morning first appears,
By the dark pole the wary Belgian steers;
Confessing now he dreads the English more
Than all the dangers of a frozen shore;
While from our arms security to find,
They fly so far, they leave the day behind.
Describe their fleet abandoning the sea,
And all their merchants left a wealthy prey;

Our first success in war make Bacchus crown,
And half the vintage of the year our own.
The Dutch their wine, and all their brandy lose,
Disarm'd of that from which their courage grows;
While the glad English, to relieve their toil,
In healths to their great leader drink the spoil.

His high command to Afric's coast extend,
And make the Moors before the English bend;
Those barb'rous pirates willingly receive
Conditions, such as we are pleased to give.
Deserted by the Dutch, let nations know
We can our own and their great business do;
False friends chastise, and common foes restrain,
Which, worse than tempests, did infest the main.
Within those Straits, make Holland's Smyrna fleet
With a small squadron of the English meet;
Like falcons these, those like a numerous flock
Of fowl, which scatter to avoid the shock.
There paint confusion in a various shape;
Some sink, some yield; and, flying, some escape.
Europe and Africa, from either shore,
Spectators are, and hear our cannon roar;
While the divided world in this agree,
Men that fight so, deserve to rule the sea.

But, nearer home, thy pencil use once more,
And place our navy by the Holland shore;
The world they compass'd, while they fought with Spain,
But here already they resign the main;

Those greedy mariners, out of whose way
Diffusive Nature could no region lay,
At home, preserved from rocks and tempests, lie,
Compell'd, like others, in their beds to die.
Their single towns th'Iberian armies press'd;
We all their provinces at once invest;
And, in a month, ruin their traffic more
Than that long war could in an age before.

But who can always on the billows lie?
The wat'ry wilderness yields no supply.
Spreading our sails, to Harwich we resort,
And meet the beauties of the British Court.
Th' illustrious Duchess, and her glorious train
(Like Thetis with her nymphs), adorn the main.
The gazing sea-gods, since the Paphian Queen
Sprung from among them, no such sight had seen.
Charm'd with the graces of a troop so fair,
Those deathless powers for us themselves declare,
Resolved the aid of Neptune's court to bring,
And help the nation where such beauties spring;
The soldier here his wasted store supplies,
And takes new valour from the ladies' eyes.

Meanwhile, like bees, when stormy winter's gone,
The Dutch (as if the sea were all their own)
Desert their ports, and, falling in their way,
Our Hamburg merchants are become their prey.
Thus flourish they, before th'approaching fight;
As dying tapers give a blazing light.

To check their pride, our fleet half-victuall'd goes,
Enough to serve us till we reach our foes;
Who now appear so numerous and bold,
The action worthy of our arms we hold.
A greater force than that which here we find,
Ne'er press'd the ocean, nor employ'd the wind.
Restrain'd a while by the unwelcome night,
Th' impatient English scarce attend the light.
But now the morning (heaven severely clear!)
To the fierce work indulgent does appear;
And Phoebus lifts above the waves his light,
That he might see, and thus record, the fight.

As when loud winds from diff'rent quarters rush,
Vast clouds encount'ring one another crush;
With swelling sails so, from their sev'ral coasts,
Join the Batavian and the British hosts.

For a less prize, with less concern and rage,
The Roman fleets at Actium did engage;
They, for the empire of the world they knew,
These, for the Old contend, and for the New.
At the first shock, with blood and powder stain'd,
Nor heaven, nor sea, their former face retain'd;
Fury and art produce effects so strange,
They trouble Nature, and her visage change.
Where burning ships the banish'd sun supply,
And no light shines, but that by which men die,
There York appears! so prodigal is he
Of royal blood, as ancient as the sea,
Which down to him, so many ages told,
Has through the veins of mighty monarchs roll'd!
The great Achilles march'd not to the field
Till Vulcan that impenetrable shield,
And arms, had wrought; yet there no bullets flew,
But shafts and darts which the weak Phrygians threw,
Our bolder hero on the deck does stand
Exposed, the bulwark of his native land;
Defensive arms laid by as useless here,
Where massy balls the neighb'ring rocks do tear.
Some power unseen those princes does protect,
Who for their country thus themselves neglect.

Against him first Opdam his squadron leads,
Proud of his late success against the Swedes;
Made by that action, and his high command,
Worthy to perish by a prince's hand.
The tall Batavian in a vast ship rides,
Bearing an army in her hollow sides;

Yet, not inclined the English ship to board,
More on his guns relies than on his sword;
From whence a fatal volley we received;
It miss'd the Duke, but his great heart it grieved;
Three worthy persons from his side it tore,
And dyed his garment with their scatter'd gore.
Happy! to whom this glorious death arrives,
More to be valued than a thousand lives!
On such a theatre as this to die,
For such a cause, and such a witness by!
Who would not thus a sacrifice be made,
To have his blood on such an altar laid?
The rest about him struck with horror stood,
To see their leader cover'd o'er with blood.
So trembled Jacob, when he thought the stains
Of his son's coat had issued from his veins.

He feels no wound but in his troubled thought;
Before, for honour, now, revenge he fought;
His friends in pieces torn (the bitter news
Not brought by Fame), with his own eyes he views.
His mind at once reflecting on their youth,
Their worth, their love, their valour, and their truth,
The joys of court, their mothers, and their wives,
To follow him abandon'd—and their lives!
He storms and shoots, but flying bullets now,
To execute his rage, appear too slow;
They miss, or sweep but common souls away;
For such a loss Opdam his life must pay.
Encouraging his men, he gives the word,
With fierce intent that hated ship to board,
And make the guilty Dutch, with his own arm,
Wait on his friends, while yet their blood is warm.
His winged vessel like an eagle shows,
When through the clouds to truss a swan she goes;

The Belgian ship unmoved, like some huge rock
Inhabiting the sea, expects the shock.
From both the fleets men's eyes are bent this way,
Neglecting all the business of the day;
Bullets their flight, and guns their noise suspend;
The silent ocean does th'event attend,
Which leader shall the doubtful victory bless,
And give an earnest of the war's success;
When Heaven itself, for England to declare,
Turns ship, and men, and tackle, into air.

Their new commander from his charge is toss'd,
Which that young prince[2] had so unjustly lost,
Whose great progenitors, with better fate,
And better conduct, sway'd their infant state.
His flight t'wards heaven th'aspiring Belgian took,
But fell, like Phaëton, with thunder strook;
From vaster hopes than his he seemed to fall,
That durst attempt the British Admiral;
From her broad sides a ruder flame is thrown
Than from the fiery chariot of the sun;
That bears the radiant ensign of the day,
And she the flag that governs in the sea.

The Duke (ill pleased that fire should thus prevent
The work which for his brighter sword he meant),
Anger still burning in his valiant breast,
Goes to complete revenge upon the rest.
So on the guardless herd, their keeper slain,

Rushes a tiger in the Libyan plain.
The Dutch, accustom'd to the raging sea,
And in black storms the frowns of heaven to see,
Never met tempest which more urged' their fears.
Than that which in the Prince's look appears.

Fierce, goodly, young! Mars he resembles, when
Jove sends him down to scourge perfidious men;
Such as with foul ingratitude have paid
Both those that led, and those that gave them aid.
Where he gives on, disposing of their fates,
Terror and death on his loud cannon waits,
With which he pleads his brother's cause so well,
He shakes the throne to which he does appeal.
The sea with spoils his angry bullets strow,
Widows and orphans making as they go;
Before his ship fragments of vessels torn,
Flags, arms, and Belgian carcasses are borne;
And his despairing foes, to flight inclined,
Spread all their canvas to invite the wind.
So the rude Boreas, where he lists to blow,
Makes clouds above, and billows fly below,
Beating the shore; and, with a boist'rous rage,
Does heaven at once, and earth, and sea engage.

The Dutch, elsewhere, did through the wat'ry field
Perform enough to have made others yield;
But English courage, growing as they fight,
In danger, noise, and slaughter, takes delight;
Their bloody task, unwearied still, they ply,
Only restrain'd by death, or victory.
Iron and lead, from earth's dark entrails torn,
Like showers of hail from either side are borne;
So high the rage of wretched mortals goes,
Hurling their mother's bowels at their foes!
Ingenious to their ruin, every age
Improves the arts and instruments of rage.
Death-hast'ning ills Nature enough has sent,
And yet men still a thousand more invent!

But Bacchus now, which led the Belgians on,
So fierce at first, to favour us begun;
Brandy and wine (their wonted friends) at length
Render them useless, and betray their strength.
So corn in fields, and in the garden flowers,
Revive and raise themselves with mod'rate showers;
But overcharged with never-ceasing rain,
Become too moist, and bend their heads again.

Their reeling ships on one another fall,
Without a foe, enough to ruin all.
Of this disorder, and the favouring wind,
The watchful English such advantage find,
Ships fraught with fire among the heap they throw,
And up the so-entangled Belgians blow.
The flame invades the powder-rooms, and then,
Their guns shoot bullets, and their vessels men.
The scorch'd Batavians on the billows float,
Sent from their own, to pass in Charon's boat.

And now, our royal Admiral success
(With all the marks of victory) does bless;
The burning ships, the taken, and the slain,
Proclaim his triumph o'er the conquer'd main.
Nearer to Holland, as their hasty flight
Carries the noise and tumult of the fight,
His cannons' roar, forerunner of his fame,
Makes their Hague tremble, and their Amsterdam;
The British thunder does their houses rock,
And the Duke seems at every door to knock.
His dreadful streamer (like a comet's hair,
Threatening destruction) hastens their despair;
Makes them deplore their scatter'd fleet as lost,
And fear our present landing on their coast.
The trembling Dutch th'approaching Prince behold,
As sheep a lion leaping tow'rds their fold;
Those piles, which serve them to repel the main,
They think too weak his fury to restrain.

'What wonders may not English valour work,
Led by th'example of victorious York?
Or what defence against him can they make,
Who, at such distance, does their country shake?
His fatal hand their bulwarks will o'erthrow,
And let in both the ocean, and the foe;'
Thus cry the people;—and, their land to keep,
Allow our title to command the deep;
Blaming their States' ill conduct, to provoke
Those arms, which freed them from the Spanish yoke.

Painter! excuse me, if I have a while
Forgot thy art, and used another style;
For, though you draw arm'd heroes as they sit,
The task in battle does the Muses fit;
They, in the dark confusion of a fight,
Discover all, instruct us how to write;
And light and honour to brave actions yield,

Hid in the smoke and tumult of the field,
Ages to come shall know that leader's toil,
And his great name, on whom the Muses smile;
Their dictates here let thy famed pencil trace,
And this relation with thy colours grace.

Then draw the Parliament, the nobles met,
And our great Monarch high above them set;
Like young Augustus let his image be,
Triumphing for that victory at sea,
Where Egypt's Queen,[3] and Eastern kings o'erthrown,
Made the possession of the world his own.
Last draw the Commons at his royal feet,
Pouring out treasure to supply his fleet;
They vow with lives and fortunes to maintain
Their King's eternal title to the main;
And with a present to the Duke, approve
His valour, conduct, and his country's love.

FOOTNOTES
[1] See History of England.
[2] 'Young prince': Prince of Orange.
[3] 'Egypt's Queen': Cleopatra.

OF ENGLISH VERSE

I
Poets may boast, as safely vain,
Their works shall with the world remain:
Both, bound together, live or die,
The verses and the prophecy.

II
But who can hope his line should long
Last in a daily changing tongue?
While they are new, envy prevails;
And as that dies, our language fails.

III
When architects have done their part,
The matter may betray their art;
Time, if we use ill-chosen stone,
Soon brings a well-built palace down.

IV
Poets that lasting marble seek,

Must carve in Latin, or in Greek;
We write in sand, our language grows,
And like the tide, our work o'erflows.

V

Chaucer his sense can only boast;
The glory of his numbers lost!
Years have defaced his matchless strain;
And yet he did not sing in vain.

VI

The beauties which adorn'd that age,
The shining subjects of his rage,
Hoping they should immortal prove,
Rewarded with success his love.

VII

This was the gen'rous poet's scope;
And all an English pen can hope,
To make the fair approve his flame,
That can so far extend their fame.

VIII

Verse, thus design'd, has no ill fate,
If it arrive but at the date
Of fading beauty; if it prove
But as long-lived as present love.

THESE VERSES WERE WRIT IN THE TASSO OF HER ROYAL HIGHNESS

Tasso knew how the fairer sex to grace,
But in no one durst all perfection place.
In her alone that owns this book is seen
Clorinda's spirit, and her lofty mien,
Sophronia's piety, Erminia's truth,
Armida's charms, her beauty, and her youth.

Our Princess here, as in a glass, does dress
Her well-taught mind, and every grace express.
More to our wonder than Rinaldo fought,
The hero's race excels the poet's thought.

THE TRIPLE COMBAT [1]

When through the world fair Mazarin had run,
Bright as her fellow-traveller, the sun,
Hither at length the Roman eagle flies,
As the last triumph of her conqu'ring eyes.
As heir to Julius, she may pretend
A second time to make this island bend;
But Portsmouth, springing from the ancient race
Of Britons, which the Saxon here did chase,
As they great Cæsar did oppose, makes head,
And does against this new invader lead.
That goodly nymph, the taller of the two,
Careless and fearless to the field does go.
Becoming blushes on the other wait,
And her young look excuses want of height.
Beauty gives courage; for she knows the day
Must not be won the Amazonian way.
Legions of Cupids to the battle come,
For Little Britain these, and those for Rome.
Dress'd to advantage, this illustrious pair
Arrived, for combat in the list appear.
What may the Fates design! for never yet
From distant regions two such beauties met.
Venus had been an equal friend to both,
And vict'ry to declare herself seems loth;
Over the camp, with doubtful wings, she flies,
Till Chloris shining in the fields she spies.
The lovely Chloris well-attended came,
A thousand Graces waited on the dame;
Her matchless form made all the English glad,
And foreign beauties less assurance had;
Yet, like the Three on Ida's top, they all
Pretend alike, contesting for the ball;
Which to determine, Love himself declined,
Lest the neglected should become less kind.
Such killing looks! so thick the arrows fly!
That 'tis unsafe to be a stander-by.
Poets, approaching to describe the fight,
Are by their wounds instructed how to write.
They with less hazard might look on, and draw
The ruder combats in Alsatia;
And, with that foil of violence and rage,
Set off the splendour of our golden age;
Where Love gives law, Beauty the sceptre sways,
And, uncompell'd, the happy world obeys.

FOOTNOTE

[1] 'Triple combat': the Duchess of Mazarin was a divorced demirep, who came to England with some
designs on Charles II., in which she was counteracted by the Duchess of Portsmouth.

UPON OUR LATE LOSS OF THE DUKE OF CAMBRIDGE [1]

The failing blossoms which a young plant bears,
Engage our hope for the succeeding years;
And hope is all which art or nature brings,
At the first trial, to accomplish things.
Mankind was first created an essay;
That ruder draught the Deluge wash'd away.
How many ages pass'd, what blood and toil,
Before we made one kingdom of this isle!
How long in vain had nature striven to frame
A perfect princess, ere her Highness came!
For joys so great we must with patience wait;
'Tis the set price of happiness complete.
As a first fruit, Heaven claim'd that lovely boy;
The next shall live, and be the nation's joy.

FOOTNOTE

[1] 'Duke of Cambridge': The Duke of York's second son by Mary d'Este. He died when he was only a month old, November 1677.

OF THE LADY MARY, PRINCESS OF ORANGE [1]

I
As once the lion honey gave,
Out of the strong such sweetness came;
A royal hero, no less brave,
Produced this sweet, this lovely dame.

II
To her the prince, that did oppose
Such mighty armies in the field,
And Holland from prevailing foes
Could so well free, himself does yield.

III
Not Belgia's fleet (his high command)
Which triumphs where the sun does rise,
Nor all the force he leads by land,
Could guard him from her conqu'ring eyes.

IV
Orange, with youth, experience has;

In action young, in council old;
Orange is, what Augustus was,
Brave, wary, provident, and bold.

V

On that fair tree which bears his name,
Blossoms and fruit at once are found;
In him we all admire the same,
His flow'ry youth with wisdom crown'd!

VI

Empire and freedom reconciled
In Holland are by great Nassau;
Like those he sprung from, just and mild,
To willing people he gives law.

VII

Thrice happy pair! so near allied
In royal blood, and virtue too!
Now love has you together tied,
May none this triple knot undo!

VIII

The church shall be the happy place
Where streams, which from the same source run,
Though divers lands a while they grace,
Unite again, and are made one.

IX

A thousand thanks the nation owes
To him that does protect us all;
For while he thus his niece bestows,
About our isle he builds a wall;

X

A wall! like that which Athens had,
By th'oracle's advice, of wood;
Had theirs been such as Charles has made,
That mighty state till now had stood.

FOOTNOTE

[1] 'Princess of Orange': The Princess Mary was married to the Prince of Orange at St. James's, in November 1677.

UPON BEN JONSON

Mirror of poets! mirror of our age!
Which her whole face beholding on thy stage,
Pleased and displeased with her own faults, endures
A remedy like those whom music cures.
Thou hast alone those various inclinations
Which Nature gives to ages, sexes, nations;
So tracèd with thy all-resembling pen,
That whate'er custom has imposed on men,
Or ill-got habit (which deforms them so,
That scarce a brother can his brother know)
Is represented to the wond'ring eyes
Of all that see, or read, thy comedies.
Whoever in those glasses looks, may find
The spots return'd, or graces, of his mind;
And by the help of so divine an art,
At leisure view, and dress, his nobler part.
Narcissus, cozen'd by that flatt'ring well,
Which nothing could but of his beauty tell,
Had here, discov'ring the deformed estate
Of his fond mind, preserved himself with hate.
But virtue too, as well as vice, is clad
In flesh and blood so well, that Plato had
Beheld, what his high fancy once embraced,
Virtue with colours, speech, and motion graced.
The sundry postures of thy copious Muse
Who would express, a thousand tongues must use;
Whose fate's no less peculiar than thy art;
For as thou couldst all characters impart,
So none could render thine, which still escapes,
Like Proteus, in variety of shapes;
Who was nor this nor that; but all we find,
And all we can imagine, in mankind.

ON MR JOHN FLETCHER'S PLAYS

Fletcher! to thee we do not only owe
All these good plays, but those of others too;
Thy wit repeated does support the stage,
Credits the last, and entertains this age.
No worthies, form'd by any Muse but thine,
Could purchase robes to make themselves so fine.

What brave commander is not proud to see
Thy brave Melantius in his gallantry?
Our greatest ladies love to see their scorn
Outdone by thine, in what themselves have worn;

Th' impatient widow, ere the year be done,
Sees thy Aspasia weeping in her gown.

I never yet the tragic strain essay'd,
Deterr'd by that inimitable Maid;[1]
And when I venture at the comic style,
Thy Scornful Lady seems to mock my toil.

Thus has thy Muse at once improved and marr'd
Our sport in plays, by rend'ring it too hard!
So when a sort of lusty shepherds throw
The bar by turns, and none the rest outgo
So far, but that the best are measuring casts,
Their emulation and their pastime lasts;
But if some brawny yeoman of the guard
Step in, and toss the axletree a yard,
Or more, beyond the furthest mark, the rest
Despairing stand; their sport is at the best.

FOOTNOTE
[1] 'Inimitable Maid': the Maid's Tragedy, the joint production of Beaumont and Fletcher.

UPON THE EARL OF ROSCOMMON'S TRANSLATION OF HORACE, 'DE ARTE POETICA;' AND OF THE USE OF POETRY

Rome was not better by her Horace taught,
Than we are here to comprehend his thought;
The poet writ to noble Piso there;
A noble Piso does instruct us here,
Gives us a pattern in his flowing style,
And with rich precepts does oblige our isle:
Britain! whose genius is in verse express'd,
Bold and sublime, but negligently dress'd.

Horace will our superfluous branches prune,
Give us new rules, and set our harp in tune;
Direct us how to back the winged horse,
Favour his flight, and moderate his force.

Though poets may of inspiration boast,
Their rage, ill-govern'd, in the clouds is lost.
He that proportion'd wonders can disclose,
At once his fancy and his judgment shows.
Chaste moral writing we may learn from hence,
Neglect of which no wit can recompense.
The fountain which from Helicon proceeds,

That sacred stream! should never water weeds,
Nor make the crop of thorns and thistles grow,
Which envy or perverted nature sow.

Well-sounding verses are the charm we use,
Heroic thoughts and virtue to infuse;
Things of deep sense we may in prose unfold,
But they move more in lofty numbers told.
By the loud trumpet, which our courage aids,
We learn that sound, as well as sense, persuades.

The Muses' friend, unto himself severe,
With silent pity looks on all that err;
But where a brave, a public action shines,
That he rewards with his immortal lines.
Whether it be in council or in fight,
His country's honour is his chief delight;
Praise of great acts he scatters as a seed,
Which may the like in coming ages breed.

Here taught the fate of verses (always prized
With admiration, or as much despised),
Men will be less indulgent to their faults,
And patience have to cultivate their thoughts.
Poets lose half the praise they should have got,
Could it be known what they discreetly blot;
Finding new words, that to the ravish'd ear
May like the language of the gods appear,
Such as, of old, wise bards employ'd, to make
Unpolish'd men their wild retreats forsake;
Law-giving heroes, famed for taming brutes,
And raising cities with their charming lutes;
For rudest minds with harmony were caught,
And civil life was by the Muses taught.
So wand'ring bees would perish in the air,
Did not a sound, proportion'd to their ear,
Appease their rage, invite them to the hive,
Unite their force, and teach them how to thrive,
To rob the flowers, and to forbear the spoil,
Preserved in winter by their summer's toil;
They give us food, which may with nectar vie,
And wax, that does the absent sun supply.

ON THE DUKE OF MONMOUTH'S EXPEDITION INTO SCOTLAND IN THE SUMMER SOLSTICE

Swift as Jove's messenger (the winged god),

With sword as potent as his charmed rod,
He flew to execute the King's command,
And in a moment reach'd that northern land,
Where day contending with approaching night,
Assists the hero with continued light.

On foes surprised, and by no night conceal'd,
He might have rush'd; but noble pity held
His hand a while, and to their choice gave space,
Which they would prove, his valour or his grace.
This not well heard, his cannon louder spoke,
And then, like lightning, through that cloud he broke.
His fame, his conduct, and that martial look,
The guilty Scots with such a terror strook,
That to his courage they resign the field,
Who to his bounty had refused to yield.
Glad that so little loyal blood it cost,
He grieves so many Britons should be lost;
Taking more pains, when he beheld them yield,
To save the flyers, than to win the field;
And at the Court his int'rest does employ,
That none, who 'scaped his fatal sword, should die.

And now, these rash bold men their error find,
Not trusting one beyond his promise kind;
One! whose great mind, so bountiful and brave,
Had learn'd the art to conquer and to save.

In vulgar breasts no royal virtues dwell;
Such deeds as these his high extraction tell,
And give a secret joy to him that reigns,
To see his blood triumph in Monmouth's veins;
To see a leader whom he got and chose,
Firm to his friends, and fatal to his foes.

But seeing envy, like the sun, does beat,
With scorching rays, on all that's high and great,
This, ill-requited Monmouth! is the bough
The Muses send to shade thy conqu'ring brow.
Lampoons, like squibs, may make a present blaze;
But time and thunder pay respect to bays.
Achilles' arms dazzle our present view,
Kept by the Muse as radiant and as new
As from the forge of Vulcan first they came;
Thousands of years are past, and they the same;
Such care she takes to pay desert with fame!
Than which no monarch, for his crown's defence,
Knows how to give a nobler recompence.

OF AN ELEGY MADE BY MRS WHARTON[1] ON THE EARL OF ROCHESTER

Thus mourn the Muses! on the hearse
Not strewing tears, but lasting verse,
Which so preserve the hero's name,
They make him live again in fame.

Chloris, in lines so like his own,
Gives him so just and high renown,
That she th'afflicted world relieves,
And shows that still in her he lives;
Her wit as graceful, great, and good;
Allied in genius, as in blood.[2]

His loss supplied, now all our fears
Are, that the nymph should melt in tears.
Then, fairest Chloris! comfort take,
For his, your own, and for our sake,
Lest his fair soul, that lives in you,
Should from the world for ever go.

FOOTNOTES

[1] 'Mrs. Wharton': the daughter, and co-heiress with the Countess of Abingdon, of Sir Henry Lee, of Ditchley, in Oxfordshire.
[2] 'In blood': the Earl of Rochester's mother was Mrs. Wharton's grand aunt.

THE LIFE OF EDMUND WALLER

It is too true, after all, that the lives of poets are not, in general, very interesting. Could we, indeed, trace the private workings of their souls, and read the pages of their mental and moral development, no biographies could be richer in instruction, and even entertainment, than those of our greater bards. The inner life of every true poet must be poetical. But in proportion to the romance of their souls' story, is often the commonplace of their outward career. There have been poets, however, whose lives are quite as readable and as instructive as their poetry, and have even shed a reflex and powerful interest on their writings. The interest of such lives has, in general, proceeded either from the extraordinary misfortunes of the bard, or from his extremely bad morals, or from his strange personal idiosyncrasy, or from his being involved in the political or religious conflicts of his age. The life of Milton, for instance, is rendered intensely interesting from his connexion with the public affairs of his critical and solemn era. The life of Johnson is made readable from his peculiar conformation of body, his bear-like manners, his oddities, and his early struggles. You devour the life of Gifford, not because he was a poet, but because he was a shoemaker; and that of Byron, more on account of his vices, his peerage, and his domestic unhappiness, than for the sake of his poetry. And in Waller, too, you feel some supplemental interest, because he united what are usually thought the incompatible characters of a poet and a political plotter, and very nearly reached the altitudes of the gallows as well as those of Parnassus.

March 1605 was the date, and Coleshill, in Hertfordshire, the place, of the birth of our poet. He was of an ancient and honourable family originally from Kent, some members of which were distinguished for their wealth and others for the valour with which, at Agincourt and elsewhere, they fought the battles of their country. Robert Waller, the poet's father, inherited from Edmund, his father, the lands of Beaconsfield, in Bucks, and other territory in Hertfordshire. These had been in 1548-9 left by Francis Waller, in default of issue by his own wife, to his brothers Thomas and Edmund, but Thomas dying, Edmund inherited the whole. Robert, on receiving his estates, quitted the profession of the law, to which he had attached himself, and spent the rest of his life chiefly at Beaconsfield, employed in the manly business and healthy amusements of a country gentleman. He died in August 1616, and left a widow and a son—the son, Edmund, being eleven years of age. It was at Beaconsfield. We need hardly remind our readers, that a far greater Edmund—Edmund Burke—spent many of his days. It was there that he composed his latest and noblest works, the "Reflections on the French Revolution," and the "Letters on a Regicide Peace;" and there he surrendered to the Creator one of the subtlest, strongest, brightest, and best of human souls. Shortly after Burke's death, the house of Beaconsfield was burnt down, and no trace of it is now, we believe, extant.

Mrs. Waller's brother, William, was the father of John Hampden. His wife, Elizabeth Cromwell, the aunt of the great Oliver, was, however, and continued to the end, a violent Royalist; and Cromwell, although he treated both her and her son with kindness, and on the terms of their relationship, was so provoked at hearing that she carried on a secret correspondence with the Stewart party, that he confined her under a very strict watch in the house of her daughter, Mrs. Price, whose husband was on the side of the Parliament. It is exceedingly probable that from the "mother's milk" of early prejudice was derived that spirit of partisanship which distinguished alike the writings and the life of the poet. It is possible, too, that contact with men so far above moral heroism and rugged mental force as Cromwell and Hampden, instead of exciting emulation, led to envy, and that his divergence from their political path sprung more from personal feeling than from principle.

He was educated, first, at the grammar school of Market, Wickham; then at Eton; and, in fine, at King's College, Cambridge. Accounts vary as to his proficiency—one Bigge, who had been his school-fellow at Wickham, told Aubrey that he never expected Waller to have become such an eminent poet, and that he used to write his exercises for him. Others, on the contrary, have alleged that it was the fame of his scholarship which led to his election for Agmondesham, a borough in Bucks, when he was only sixteen years of age. This story, so far as his premature learning goes, seems rather apocryphal; but certain it is, that when scarcely eighteen, he had become M.P. for the above-mentioned borough. The parliament in which he found himself, was one of those subservient and cringing assemblies which James I. was wont to summon to sit till they had voted the supplies, and then contemptuously to dismiss. It met in November 1621, and after passing a resolution in support of their privileges, which James tore out of the Journals with his own hand, and granting the usual supplies, was dissolved on the 6th of January 1622. Waller was probably as silent and servile as any of his neighbours. He began, however, to feel his way as a courtier, and overheard some curious and not very canonical talk of James with his lords and bishops, the record of which reminds you of some of the richer scenes of the "Fortunes of Nigel." The next parliament was not called till 1624, when Waller was not elected. The electors of Agmondesham, who had, meantime, obtained fuller privileges, chose two matured members to represent them, and the precocious boy lost his seat.

Waller's "political and poetical life began nearly together." It was in his eighteenth year that he wrote his first poetical piece—that on the escape of Prince Charles from a tempest on his return from Spain. It is a tissue of smooth and musical mediocrity. It shews a kind of stunted prematurity. The perfection which is attained by a single effort is generally a poor and tame one. This poem of Waller's, like several of his others, has all that merit which arises from the absence of fault, and all that fault which arises from the absence of merit—of high poetic merit, we mean, for in music it is equal to any of his poems. Much has been said about the model which he followed in his versification, the majority of critics tracing in it an imitation of Fairfax's Tasso. The fact seems to be that Waller, with a good ear, had a very limited theory of verse. He worshipped smoothness, and sought it at every hazard. He preferred the Jacob of a soft flowing commonplace to the rough hairy Esau of a strong originality, cumbered with its own weight and richness. We think that this excessive love of the soft, and horror at the rude, materially weakened his genius. The true theory of versification lies in variety, and in accommodation to the necessities and fluctuations of the thought. The "Paradise Lost," written in Waller's rhyme, would have been as ridiculous as Waller's love to Saccharissa expressed in Milton's blank verse. The school before Waller were too rugged, but surely there is a medium between the roughness of Donne, and the honied monotony of the author of the "Summer Islands." The practice of running the lines into one another, severely condemned by Johnson, and systematically shunned by Waller, has often been practised with success by poets far greater than either—such as Shelley and Coleridge. It is remarkable that Dryden, while he praised, did not copy our poet's manner, but gave himself freer scope. Pope, on the other hand, pushed his love of uniform tinkle and unmitigated softness to excess, and transferred this kind of luscious verse from small poems, where it is often a merit, to large ones, where it is a mistake. In his "Iliad," for instance, the fierce ire of Achilles, the dignified resentment of Agamemnon, the dull courage of Ajax, the chivalrous sentiment of Hector, the glowing energy of Diomede, the veteran wisdom of Nestor, the grief of Andromache, the love of Helen, the jealousy of Juno, and the godlike majesty of Jupiter, are all expressed in the same sweet and monotonous melody—a verse called "heroic," by courtesy, or on the principle of contradiction, like lucus a non lucendo. In Waller, however, his poems being all, without exception, rather short, you never think of quarrelling with his uniformity of manner; and rise from his lines as from a liberal feast of hot-house grapes, thankful, but feeling that a few more would have turned satisfaction into nausea. Yet you feel, too, that perhaps his selection of small themes, and the consequent curbing of his powers, have sprung from his fastidiousness in the matter of versification. The sermons, the satires, the speeches, the odes, and the didactic poems of the fastidious are generally short, and do not, therefore, fully mirror the amplitude, or express the energy of their genius. To his poem on the escape of Prince Charles, succeeded that on the Prince, and two or three others of a similar kind; all finding their inspiration, not as yet in that love of others which animated his amatory effusions, but in that love to himself and his own interest which marks the incipient courtier, who is beginning, in Shakspeare's thought, to hang his knee upon "hinges," that it may bend more readily to power. Yet his case shews that there is a certain incompatibility between the profession of a courtier and that of a poet. He often began his panegyrics with much fervour, but the fit passed, or his fastidious taste produced disgust at what he had written, and it was either not finished, or was delayed till the interest of the occasion had passed away.

After the death of James I., Charles called a new parliament in 1625, and in it Waller took his place for Chipping-Wycombe, a borough in Buckinghamshire. This parliament met in London, but was adjourned to Oxford on account of the Plague. In Oxford, it proved refractory to the king's wishes, and refusing to grant him a tithe of the supplies which he demanded, was summarily dismissed. Waller was not re-elected in 1626, when the next parliament was summoned, but secured his return for Agmondesham in March 1627. He appears to have been in these years a silent senator, taking little interest or share in the debates, but retiring from them to offer the quit-rent of his versicles—a laureate without salary, and yet not probably much more sincere than laureates generally are; for although his loyalty was undoubted, his expressions of it in rhyme are often hyperbolical to a degree.

In his twenty-sixth year, he married an heiress, the daughter of Mr. Banks, a wealthy London citizen. In this there was nothing singular but the fact, that he, as yet obscure, distanced a rival of great influence, whose suit was supported by royalty—namely, Mr. Crofts, afterwards Baron Crofts—gave rather a romantic and adventurous air to the match. He retired soon after to Beaconsfield, where he spent some happy years in the enjoyment of domestic society, pursuing, too, his studies under the direction of Morley, afterwards Bishop of Winchester, a distinguished scholar of the time, who resided with him. During this period he is said to have read many poets, but to have written little poetry. Although the king, jealous of his subjects, had, in 1632, by a most absurd and arbitrary decree, commanded all the lords and gentry in the kingdom to reside on their own estates, Waller did not at the time consider this an exceeding hardship. Indeed, his feelings were on no subject, and under no pressure of circumstances, either very profound or very lasting.

His wife died after having borne him a son and a daughter—a son, who did not long survive his mother; and a daughter, who became afterwards Mrs. Dormer of Oxfordshire. From under this calamity Waller, yet only thirty years of age, rebounded with characteristic elasticity. He came back, nothing both, to the society he had left, and was soon known to be in quest of a fair lady, whom he has made immortal by the sobriquet of Saccharissa. She was the eldest daughter of the Earl of Leicester, and her name was the Lady Dorothy Sidney. This lady was counted beautiful. Her father was absent in foreign parts. She lived almost alone in Penshurst. It added to her charms, at least in a poetical eye, that she was descended from Sir Philip Sidney; a man whose name, as the flower of chivalry and the soul of honour, is still "like ointment poured forth" in the estimation of the world—whose death rises almost to the dignity and grandeur of a martyrdom—and who has left in his "Arcadia" a quaintly decorated, conceived, and unequally chiselled, but true, rich, and magnificent monument of his genius. In spite, however, of all Waller's tender ditties, of the incense he offered up—not only to Dorothy, but to her sister Lady Lucy, and even to her maid Mrs. Braughton—his goddess was inexorable, and not only rejected, but spurned him from her feet. The poet bore this disappointment, as all poets, Dante hardly excepted, have borne the same: he transferred his affections to another, who, indeed, ere Saccharissa-like the sun had set in the west, had risen like the moon in the east of her lover's admiration, and soon, although only for a short time, possessed the sky alone. This was his Amoret, who is said to have been Lady Sophia Murray. The Juliet, however, was not one whit more placable than the Rosalind— she, too, rejected his suit; and this rejection threw Waller, not into despair or melancholy, but into a wide sea of miscellaneous flirtations, with we know not how many Chlorises, Sylvias, Phyllises, and Flavias, all which names stood, it seems, for real persons, and testified to a universality in the poet's affections which is rather ludicrous than edifying. His heart was as soft, and shallower than his verse.

Saccharissa married Lord Spencer, afterwards the Earl of Sunderland, who was killed at the battle of Newbury. After his death, she was united to a Mr. Robert Smythe; and she now lies at Brinton, in Northamptonshire, while her picture continues, from the walls of the gallery at Penshurst, to shed down the soft, languishing, and voluptuous smile which had captivated the passions, if it could hardly be said to have really touched the heart, of her poetical admirer. He not very long after his twofold rejection, consoled himself by marrying a second wife. Her name was Breaux or Bresse; and all we know of her is, that she bore and brought up a great many children.

In 1639, the urgencies of the times compelled Charles to call a new parliament, and it was decreed that politics instead of love and song should now for a time engross our poet. And there opened up to him unquestionably a noble field of patriotic exertion had he been fully adapted for its cultivation—his firmness been equal to his eloquence, and his sincerity to his address—had he been more of a Whig in the good old Hampden sense, and less of a trimmer. As it is, he cuts, on the whole, a doubtful figure, and is no great favourite with the partisans of either of the great contending parties. He was again elected member for Agmondesham, and when the question came before the House, whether the supplies demanded by Strafford should be granted, or the grievances complained of by the Commons should be first redressed, he delivered an oration, trying with considerable dexterity to steer a medium course between the two sides. In this speech, while contending for the constitutional principle advocated by the Commons, and expressing great attachment to his Majesty's person, he maintained that the chief blame of the king's obnoxious measures lay with his clerical advisers, and concluded by moving that the House should first consider the grievances, and then grant the royal demand. Charles, who had personally requested Waller to second the motion for instantly granting the supplies, was not, we imagine, particularly pleased with his "volunteer" laureate's conduct; and his temporary defection did not tend to allay the royal fury at the parliament, which burst out forthwith in an act of sudden and wrathful dismissal.

This session, called from its extreme brevity the Short Parliament, ended in May. In November met that memorable assembly, destined not to separate till it had outlived a monarchy and a hierarchy, and seen a brewer's son take the sceptre instead of the descendant of a hundred kings, the Long Parliament. Waller, again member for Agmondesham, had made himself popular by his speech in the beginning of the year, and was chosen by the Commons to manage the prosecution of Judge Crawley for advising the levy of ship-money. He conducted the case with talent, acuteness, and moderation. Soon after, however, as the gulph widened between the king and the parliament, his position became extremely awkward. His understanding on the whole was with the parliament, although he did not approve of some of their measures, but his heart was with the royal cause. He first of all, along with a others (whose example was imitated by Fox and his party during the French Revolution), retired from parliament, but in consequence of the permission or request of the king, he speedily resumed his seat. When Charles put himself in a warlike attitude in August 1642, Waller sent him a present of a thousand broad pieces. Still his plausible language, the tone of moderation which he preserved, and his connexion with Cromwell and Hampden, rendered the popular party unwilling to believe him a traitor to their cause, and he was appointed, after the battle at Edgehill, one of the commissioners who met at Oxford to treat of peace. Here, it is said, that one of those compliments which cost the subtle Charles so little (Waller was last in being presented to the king, and his Majesty told him, "Though last, you are not the lowest nor the least in my favour"), gained over Waller, and suggested to him the scheme of his famous plot. We do not think so little of our hero's intellect, or so much of his heart, as to credit this story. Though not aged, he was by far too old to be caught with such chaff. He knew, too, before, Charles' private sentiments towards him, and we incline with some of his biographers to suppose that these words of royalty were simply the signal to Waller to fire the train which the king knew right well had already been prepared.

Poets are in general poor politicians and miserable plotters. They seldom, even in verse or fiction, manage a state plot well. Scott, at least, has completely failed in his treatment of the Popish plot in "Peveril," and they always bungle it in reality. They are either too unsuspicious or too scheming, too shallow or too profound. That mixture of transparency and craft, of simplicity and subtlety, requisite to all deep schemes, and which Poe (himself a confused compound of the genius, the simpleton, and the scoundrel) has so admirably exemplified in the "Purloined Letter," is not often competent to men of imagination and impulse. Waller was not a very creative spirit; but here he was true to his class, and failed like a very poet. He had a brother-in-law named Tomkins, clerk of the Queen's Council, and possessed of much influence in the city. Consulting together on national affairs, it struck them simultaneously that energetic measures might yet save the court. They saw, or thought they saw, a reaction in favour of the royal cause, and they determined to try and unite the royalists together in a peaceful but strong combination against the parliament. They appointed confidential agents to make out, in the different parishes and wards, lists of those persons who were or were not friendly to their cause; and to secure secrecy, they prohibited more than three of their party from meeting in one place, and no individual was to reveal the design to more than two others. Lord Conway, fresh from Ireland, joined the confederacy, and probably the counsels of such an ardent soldier served to modify the original purpose, and to give it a military colour. Meanwhile, Sir Nicholas Crispe, a bolder spirit than Waller, had organised a different scheme in favour of Charles. He had, when a merchant in the city, procured a loan of £100,000 for the king; he had then raised and taken the command of a regiment; he had obtained from Charles a commission of array, which Lady Aubigny, ignorant of its contents, was to deliver to a gentleman in London. Crispe's plan was bold and comprehensive. He intended to remove the king's children to a place of safety, to enlist soldiers, collect magazines, and raise monies by contribution, to release the prisoners committed by the parliament, to arrest some of the leading members in both Houses, to issue declarations, and whenever the conspiracy was ripe, to raise flags at Temple Bar, the Exchange, and other central spots.

It was impossible that two such plots could escape collision with each other—or that either should be long concealed. On the 31st May 1643, a fast-day, Pym is seated in St. Margaret's Church, hearing sermon. A messenger enters and gives him a letter. He reads hastily—communicates its intelligence in whispers to those beside him, and hurries out. No time is lost. Pym and his party could not trifle now though they would, and would not though they could. Waller and Tomkins are seized that night in their houses, and overwhelmed with fear, confess everything. It is suspected that Waller was betrayed by his sister, Mrs. Price, who was married to a zealous parliamentarian. A strange story is told, that one Goode, her chaplain, had stolen some of his papers, and would have got a hold of them all, had not Waller, having DREAMED that his sister was perfidious, risen and secured the rest. Clarendon, on the other hand, says that the discovery was made by a servant of Tomkins, who acted as a spy for the parliament. At all events, they were found out, and, in their terror and pusillanimity, they betrayed their associates. The Duke of Portland and Lord Conway were instantly arrested. Lady Aubigny, too, was imprisoned, but contrived to make her escape to the Hague. Even the Earl of Northumberland was involved in the charges which now issued in a trembling torrent from the lips of the detected conspirator, who confessed a great deal that could not have been discovered, and offered to reveal the private conversations of ladies of rank, and to betray all and sundry who were in the slightest degree connected with the plot. Tomkins had somehow got possession of Crispe's commission of array, which he had buried in the garden, but which was now, on his information, dug up. Never did a conspiracy fall to pieces more rapidly, completely, and, for the conspirators, more disgracefully.

This discovery proves a windfall to the parliamentary party. Pym hies to the citizens and apprises them, in one breath, at once of their danger and their signal deliverance. The Commons draw up a vow and covenant, expressing their detestation of all such conspiracies, and appoint a day of thanksgiving for the escape of the nation. Meanwhile Waller and Portland are confronted, when the one repeats his charge and Portland denies it. Conway, too, maintains his innocence, and as Waller is the only evidence against either him or Portland, both are, after a long imprisonment, admitted to bail. Tomkins, Chaloner (the agent of Crispe), Hassel (the king's courier between Oxford and London), Alexander Hampden (Waller's cousin), and some subordinate conspirators, are arraigned before a Council of War. Waller feigns himself so ill with remorse of conscience, that his trial is put off that he "may recover his understanding." Hassel dies the night before the trial. Tomkins and Chaloner are hanged before their own doors. Hampden escapes punishment, but is retained in prison, where he dies; and the subordinates just referred to (Blinkorne and White) are pardoned. Northumberland, owing to his rank, is only once examined before the Lords. Those whose names were inserted in the commission of array are treated as malignants, and their estates seized.

Waller, having received some respite, employed the time in petitioning, flattering, bribing, confessing, beseeching, and in the exercise of every other art by which a mean, cowardly spirit seeks to evade death. He appealed from the military jurisdiction to the House of Commons, and was admitted to plead his cause at their bar. His speech was humble, conciliating, and artful, but failed to gain the object. He was expelled from the House, and soon after was sisted before the Court of War, and condemned to die. He was reprieved, however, by Essex, and at the end of a year's imprisonment, the sentence was commuted into a fine of £10,000, and banishment for life. He was sent to "recollect himself in another country." He had previously expended, it is said, £30,000 in bribes.

Waller's conduct in this whole matter was a mixture of cowardice and meanness. Recollecting his poetical temperament, and the well-known stories of Demosthenes at Cheronea, and Horace at Philippi, we are not disposed to be harsh on his cowardice, but we have no excuse for his meanness. It discovers a want of heart, and an infinite littleness of soul. We can hardly conceive him to have possessed a drop of the blood of Hampden or Cromwell in his veins, and cease to wonder why two high-spirited ladies of rank should have spurned the homage of a poetic poltroon, whom instinctively they seem to have known to be such, even before he proved it to the world.

"Infamous, and not contented," Waller repairs to the Continent, first to Rouen, then to Switzerland and Italy, in company with his friend Evelyn, and, in fine, settles for a season in Paris. Here he keeps open table for the banished royalists, as well as for the French wits, till his means are impaired by his liberality. A middling poet, a pitiful politician, a fickle dangler in affairs of love, Waller was an admirable host, and not only gave good dinners and suppers, but flavoured them delicately with compliment and repartee. In Paris he recovered his tone of spirits, and, had his money lasted, might have remained there till his dying day. But fines and bribes had exhausted his patrimony, and he was compelled first to sell a property in Bedfordshire, worth more than £1,000 a-year, then to part with his wife's jewels, and in fine to sell the last of these, which he called "the rump jewel." His family, too, had increased, and added to his incumbrances. His favourite was a daughter, Margaret, born in Rouen, who acted as his amanuensis. At last, through the intercession of his brother-in-law, Scroope, he was permitted to return to England. This was on the 13th of January 1652. During all his residence on the Continent, he had continued to amuse himself with poetry, "in which," says Johnson, "he sometimes speaks of the rebels and their usurpation, in the natural language of an honest man." If this mean that Waller, when he uttered such sentiments, was, for the nonce, sincere, it is quite true; but if the Doctor means that Waller was, speaking generally, an honest man, it is not true; and Dr. Johnson repeatedly signifies, in other parts of his life, that he does not believe it to be true. He speaks, for instance, of the "exorbitance of his adulation," of his "having lost the esteem of all parties," and says, "It is not possible to read without some contempt and indignation, poems ascribing the highest degree of power and piety to Charles the First, and then transferring the same power and piety to Oliver Cromwell." In keeping with this, Bishop Burnet asserts, that "in the House he was only concerned to say what should make him applauded, and never laid the business of the House to heart."

Waller, returning, found his mother still alive at Beaconsfield, where Cromwell sometimes visited her; and when she talked in favour of the royal cause, would throw napkins at her, and say that he would not dispute with his aunt, although afterwards, as we have seen, her spirit of political intrigue compelled him to make her a prisoner in her own house. The poet took up his residence near her at Hall-barn, a house of his own erection, and on the walls of which he hung up a picture of Saccharissa, whence he hoped, it may be, draw consolation for the past, and inspiration for the future. Here Cromwell, who probably despised Waller in his heart, as often men of action despise men of mere literary ability, especially when that ability is not transcendent, but whose cue it was to conciliate all men according to their respective positions and capabilities, paid great attention to his kinsman. Waller found Cromwell well acquainted with the ancient historians, and they conversed a good deal on such topics. It is said, that when Waller jeered him on his using the peculiar phraseology of the Puritans in his conversation with them, the Protector answered, "Cousin Waller, I must talk to these men in their own way;" an anecdote which is sometimes quoted as if it proved that Cromwell had no religion; whereas it only proved that he had at heart no cant. It was not as if he had privately avowed infidelity to his kinsman. Cromwell found cant prevalent on his stage, just as any great actor of that century found rant on his, and, like the actor, he used it occasionally as a means of gaining his own lofty ends, and as a foil to his own genuine earnestness and power.

The Protector, however, seems to have profoundly impressed even Waller's light and fickle mind; and the panegyric which he produced on him in 1654, is not only the ablest, but seems the sincerest of his productions. He had hitherto been writing about women, courtiers, and kings; but now he had to gird up his loins and write on a man. The piece is accordingly as masculine in style, as it is just in appreciation; and, with the exception of Milton's glorious sketch in the "Defensio pro populo Anglicano," and Carlyle's lecture in his "Heroes and Hero-worship," it is, perhaps, the best encomium ever pronounced on the Lord Protector of England—almost worthy of Cromwell's unrivalled merits and achievements, and more than worthy of Waller's powers. It is said, that when twitted with having written a better panegyric on Cromwell than a congratulation to Charles II., he wittily replied, "You should remember that poets succeed better in fiction than in truth." Perhaps in this he spoke ironically; certainly the fact was the reverse of his words. It is because he has spoken truth in the first, and fiction in the second, of productions, that the first is incomparably the better poem. Sketches of character taken from the life are better than those where imagination operates on hearsays and on recorded actions. And certainly few men had a better opportunity than Waller of seeing in private and in undress, and with an eye in which native sagacity was sharpened by prejudices, partly for, partly against, the Man of that century—a man in whom we recognise a union of Roman, Hebrew, and English qualities—the faith of the Jew, the firmness of the Roman, and the homespun simplicity of the Englishman of his own age—in purpose and in powers "an armed angel on a battle-day;" in manners a plain blunt corporal; and in language always a stammerer, and sometimes a buffoon; the middle-class man of his time, with the merits and the defects of his order, but touched with an inspiration as from heaven, lifting him far above all the aristocracy, and all the royalty, and all the literature of his period; who found his one great faculty—inflamed and consecrated commonsense—to be more than equal to the subleties, and brilliancies, and wit, and eloquence, and taste, and genius, of his thousand opponents—whose crown was a branch of English oak, his sceptre a strong sapling of the same, his throne a mound of turf—who economised matters by being at once king and king's jester, and whose mere clenched fist, held up at home or across the waters, saved millions of money, awed despots, encouraged freedom in every part of the world, and had nearly established a pure form of Christianity over Great Britain—who gave his country a model of excellence as a man, and as a ruler, simple, severe, ruggedly picturesque, and stupendously original, and solitary as one of the primitive rocks—whose eloquence was uneven and piercing as the forked lightning, which is never so terrible as when it falls to pieces—and highest praise of all, whose deeds and character were so great in their sublime simplicity, that the poet, who afterwards sung the hierarchies of heaven, and the anarchies of hell, was fain to sit a humble secretary, recording the thoughts and actions of Cromwell, and felt afterwards that he had been as nobly employed when defending his grand defiance of evil and arbitrary power, as when he did

"Assert Eternal Providence,
And justify the ways of God to man."

We have seen pictured representations of Cromwell and Milton seated together at the council-table, in which the painter wished more than to insinuate that Milton was the superior being; but in our judgment the advantage was on the other side, and the poet seemed to bear only that relation and proportion to the Protector which the eloquent Raphael, the "affable archangel," the bard of the war in heaven, does to the Gabriel or the Michael, whose tremendous sword mingled in and all but decided the fray. And we thought what a junction were that of the two powers—of the sword and the pen, the actor and the recorder, the man to do, and the poet to sing! Waller in his panegyric sees and shews in a few lines Cromwell's relation to Britain, and that of both to the world:—

"Heaven that has placed this island to give law,
To balance Europe, and her states to awe,
In this conjunction does on Britain smile,
The greatest leader and the greatest isle."

He saw that in Cromwell, and in Cromwell alone, had the power of Britain come to a point: IT was made, if not to be the governor to be the moderator of the earth, and HE was sent to govern it, to condense its scattered energies, to awe down its warring factions, and to wield all its forces to one good and great end. In him for the first time had the wild island, the Bucephalus of the West, found a rider able, by backing, bridling, and curbing him, to give due direction and momentum to his fury, force, and speed.

He has scattered some other precious particles of thought in this poem, such as:—

"Lords of the world's great waste, the ocean, we
Whole forests send to reign upon the sea."

"The Caledonians, arm'd with want and cold."

"The states, changed by you,
Changed like the world's great scene, when without noise,
The rising sun night's vulgar lights destroys."

"Illustrious acts high raptures do infuse,
And every conqueror creates a Muse."

When Cromwell died, Waller again lifted up his pen, and indited a short lamentation over his loss. After the Restoration, he was one of the first to read a poetical recantation of his errors in verses addressed to Charles II. In 1661 he was returned to parliament for Hastings, in Sussex, and sat afterwards at various times for Chipping-Wycombe, and Saltash. In parliament, he was rather famed for his lively sallies of wit, than for his logic, sense, or earnestness. In private, his spirits, even without the aid of wine,—which he never drank,—continued to a great age unusually buoyant. As he advanced in life he became more religious, and intermixed a vein of devotion with his verse. When eighty-two, he bought a small estate in Coleshill, near his native place, desirous, he said, "to die, like the stag, where he was roused." His wish, however, was not granted. Seized with tumours in his legs, he went to Windsor to consult Sir Charles Scarborough, then waiting on the king. Sir Charles, at Waller's request to know the "meaning" of these swellings, told him that they showed that his "blood would no longer run." On this the poet quietly repeated a passage from Virgil, and returned to Beaconsfield to die. Having received the sacrament, and shared it with his children, and expressed his faith in Christianity, he expired on the 21st of October 1687. He was buried in the churchyard of Beaconsfield. He left five sons and eight daughters. His eldest son being an imbecile, Edmund, his second, inherited the estates, and having joined the party of the Prince of Orange, sat for Agmondesham for some years, but became ultimately a Quaker. The fortunes of the rest of his family are not particularly interesting, and need not be related.

As a character, our opinion of Waller has been already indicated. He was indecisive, vacillating, with more wit than judgment, and with more judgment than earnestness. In that age of high hearts, stormy passions, and determined purpose, he looks helpless and not at home, like a butterfly in an eagle's eyrie. A gifted, accomplished, and apparently an amiable man, he was a feeble, and almost a despicable character. The parliament seem to have thought him hardly worth hanging. Cromwell bore with him only as a kinsman, and respected him only as a scholar. Charles II. liked to laugh at his jokes, and to Saville his company was as good as an additional bottle of wine. His only chance of fame as a man of action arose from his connexion with the plot, which, however, in its issue covered him with infamy, as all bad things bungled, inevitably do to those who attempt them.

Although he unquestionably in some points improved our correctness of style and our versification, there is not much to be said either for or against his poetry. It is as a whole a mass of smooth and easy, yet systematic, trifling. Nine-tenths of it does not rise above mediocrity, and the tenth that remains is more distinguished by grace than by grandeur or depth. His lines on Cromwell we have already characterised. It may seem odd, but in his verses on the head of a stag, which Johnson singles out as bad, we see more of the soul of poetry than in any of his other productions.

Let our readers, if they will not be convinced by our assertion, listen to some of these lines:—

"So we some antique hero's strength,
Learn by his lance's weight and length—
As these vast beams express the beast
Whose shady brows alive they dress'd.
Such game, while yet the world was new,
The mighty Nimrod did pursue;
What huntsman of our feeble race
Or dogs dare such a monster chase?
*　　*　　*　　*　　*
Oh, fertile head, which every year
Could such a CROP of WONDER bear!"

In his amorous and complimentary ditties, he is often very successful. So, too, is he in much of his "Divine Poetry," particularly the lines at the end, beginning with—

"The soul's dark cottage, batter'd and decay'd,"
Lets in new light through chinks which time hath made.

These contain a thought, so far as we remember, new and highly poetical.

We may close by saying a few words on a question which Dr. Johnson has started in his "Life of Waller" in reference to sacred poetry. That great and good man, our readers remember, maintains that the ideas of the Christian theology are too simple for eloquence, too sacred for fiction, and too majestic for ornament, and "that faith, thanksgiving, repentance, and supplication," are all unsusceptible of poetical treatment. He grants that the doctrines of religion may be defended in a didactic poem, and that a poet may not only describe God's works in nature, but may trace them up to nature's God. But he asserts that "contemplative piety, or the intercourse between God and the human soul, cannot be poetical." It is curious to remember that, up to Johnson's time, the best poetry in the world had been sacred. There had been the poetry of the Bible, in which truth of the deepest import was expressed, now in "eloquence," now in "fiction," and now in language most gorgeously "ornamented," and in which "Faith" in Isaiah, "Thanksgiving" in Moses, "Penitence" in David, and "Supplication" in Jeremiah, had uttered themselves in sublime, or lively, or subdued, or tender strains —the poetry of the "Divine Commedia," of the "Jerusalem Delivered," of the "Faery Queen," of the "Paradise Lost" and "Paradise Regained," of the "Night-Thoughts," of "Smart's David," all poetry, let it be observed, not defending religion merely, or confining itself to the praise of God's lower works, but entering into the depths of divine contemplation, into the very adyta of the heavenly temple. And it is no less interesting to recollect that in spite of Dr. Johnson's sage diction, sacred poetry of a very high order has, since his day, abounded. Cowper has extracted it from "the intercourse between God and the human soul;" Montgomery has made now "the supplication," and now the "thanksgiving," of the poor negro ring in every ear, and vibrate through every heart; Coleridge has expressed, in his sounding and splendid measures, at one time his "faith," and at another his "repentance;" Pollok has with true, although unequal steps, followed Milton and Dante, both into the heaven of heavens, and into the gloom of Gehenna; and Wordsworth, Southey, Croly, Milman, Trench, Keble, and a host more have, by their noble religious hymns, shamed the wisdom of the Sadducee, and darkened the glory of the song of the sceptic. Why argue about principles while we can appeal to facts? Why shew either the probabilities against, or the probabilities for, good sacred poetry, while we see it before us, gushing from a thousand springs, and gladdening every corner of the church and of the world?

Dr. Johnson says, "Whatever is great, desirable, or tremendous, is comprised in the name of the Supreme Being. Omnipotence cannot be exalted. Infinity cannot be amplified. Perfection cannot be improved." All this is as true as it is pointedly expressed; but though true, it is nothing to the purpose— nay, bears as much against prayer as against poetry. What meant the Psalmist when he said, "My soul doth magnify the Lord?" Did he aspire to exalt Omnipotence or to amplify perfection? No; but only first to shew his own feeling of their magnitude; and, again, to raise himself a step toward an approximately adequate conception of the Most High. So in religious poetry. We cannot add to, or exalt God, but we can raise ourselves up nearer to Him, and attain, if not a full understanding, a deeper feeling of the elements of His surpassing excellence and glory. Indeed, as the highest poetry (in Milton, for instance) blossoms into prayer, so the truest prayer, often by insensible gradation, becomes poetry.

Dr. Johnson says, that "of sentiments purely religious, the most simple expression is the most sublime." True, and hence, the best religious poetry is at once sublime and simple. He adds, "Poetry loses its lustre and its power, because it is applied to the decoration of something more excellent than itself." On this principle, poets should never sing of God's works in nature—of the ocean, or the sun, or the stars—no, nor of the heroic achievements of man's courage, or of the self-sacrifices of his love—for are not all these more excellent than poetry? Dr Johnson's theory would hush the "New Song" itself, and perpetuate that silence which was once in heaven "for half-an-hour."

Long before the Doctor vented this paradox, Cowley, in his preface to his poems, had written the following eloquent and memorable sentences on this subject:—"When I consider how many bright and magnificent subjects Scripture affords, and proffers, as it were, to poesy, in the wise managing and illustrating whereof the glory of God Almighty might be joined with the singular utility and noblest delight of mankind, it is not without grief and indignation that I behold that divine science employing all her inexhaustible riches of wit and eloquence, either in the wicked and beggarly flattering of great persons, or the unmanly idolising of foolish women, or the wretched affectation of scurril laughter, or the confused dreams of senseless fables and metamorphoses. Amongst all holy and consecrated things which the devil ever stole and alienated from the service of the Deity—as altars, temples, sacrifices, prayers, and the like—there is none that he so universally and so long usurped as poetry. It is time to recover it out of the tyrant's hands, and to restore it to the kingdom of God, who is the Father of it. It is time to baptize it in Jordan, for it will never become clean by bathing in the waters of Damascus.

"What can we imagine more proper for the ornaments of wit and learning in the story of Deucalion than in that of Noah? Why will not the actions of Samson afford as plentiful matter as the Labours of Hercules? (Perhaps from this Milton took the hint of writing his "Samson Agonistes.") Why is not Jephtha's daughter as good a woman as Iphigenia? and the friendship of David and Jonathan more worthy celebration than that of Theseus and Pirithous? Does not the passage of Moses and the Israelites into the Holy Land yield incomparably more poetic variety than the voyages of Ulysses and Aeneas? Are the obsolete, threadbare tales of Thebes and Troy half so well stored with great, heroical, and supernatural actions (since verse will needs find or make such), as the wars of Joshua, of the Judges, of David, and divers others? Can all the transformations of the gods give such copious hints to flourish and expatiate on as the true miracles of Christ, or of His prophets and apostles? What do I instance in these few particulars? All the books in the Bible are either already most admirable and exalted pieces of poetry, or are the best materials in the world for it.

"Yet," he adds with great judiciousness, "though they be so proper in themselves to be made use of for this purpose, none but a good artist will know how to do it, neither must we think to cut and polish diamonds with so little pains and skill as we do marble. He who can write a profane poem well, may write a divine one better; but he who can do that but ill, will do this much worse, and so far from elevating poesy will but abase divinity. The same fertility of invention—the same wisdom of disposition—the same judgment in observance of decencies—the same lustre and vigour of elocution— the same modesty and majesty of number— briefly, the same kind of habit—is required in both, only this latter allows better stuff, and therefore would look more deformedly drest in it."

The errors of a great author are often more valuable than his sound sentiments; because they tend, by the reaction they provoke, and the replies they elicit, to dart new light upon the opposite truths. And so it has been with this dogma of the illustrious Lexicographer. It has led to some admirable rejoinders from such pens as those of Montgomery, and of Christopher North, which have not only rebutted Johnson's objections, but have directed public attention more strongly to the general theme, and served to shed new light upon the nature and province of religious poetry.

www.ingramcontent.com/pod-product-compliance
Lightning Source LLC
Chambersburg PA
CBHW060135050426
42448CB00010B/2133